WEST COAST VICTORIANS

WEST COAST VICTORIANS

A Nineteenth-Century Legacy

Kenneth Naversen

Beautiful America Publishing Co.
9725 S.W. Commerce Circle
Wilsonville, OR 97070

All rights reserved.
© Copyright 1987 by Kenneth Naversen

Design and Layout: Carla Laurent

Typesetting: Arrow Connection

Printing: Hong Kong

Second Printing

Library of Congress Cataloging-in-Publication Data

Naversen, Kenneth, 1944–
  West Coast Victorians.

  Bibliography: p.
  Includes index.
  1. Architecture, Domestic—Pacific Coast (U.S.)
2. Architecture, Victorian—Pacific Coast (U.S.)
3. Architecture, Modern—19th century—Pacific
Coast (U.S.) I. Title.
NA7225.N38   1987   728′.0970   87-17426

ISBN: 0-89802-494-3 (paper)

ISBN: 0-89802-495-1 (cloth)

To Kristina

Table of Contents

Introduction

The Victorian era in architecture corresponds closely with the final wave of national expansion that carried American gold seekers and settlers to the shores of the Pacific in the last half of the 19th century. This book is about some of the houses of that period and that region, but it is not a history or even a guide. It is, more humbly, a sort of catalogue. Its primary emphasis is photographic, and its basic purpose is to provide a pictorial sampling of some of the Victorian domestic architecture that has managed to survive to the present on the West Coast. Beyond this it also hopes to suggest some of the ways these houses were woven into the social and economic fabric of the era.

As an inventory, of course, the book is necessarily selective and incomplete. Of the many Victorian houses that are still with us in California, Oregon, and Washington, only a relatively small number could realistically be fitted into this single volume. So the basic editorial problem—what to include and what to leave out—loomed large from the very beginning of the project. In trying to answer this question I have adopted a somewhat middle-of-the-road approach: on the one hand I felt it important to include as many *bona fide* landmarks of the era as possible (as much for the influence they had on smaller, more modest dwellings as for their own intrinsic merit). But I have also tried to leave room for examples that seemed especially representative of particular architectural styles or geographic locales. Also, for one reason or another, it seemed desirable to emphasize some communities and underplay others. Some of this is simply a reflection of what's out there. As might be expected, towns that have managed to retain significant numbers of Victorians have received more attention than those whose architectural wealth belongs to other eras. But in some cases the editorial knife may seem to have been wielded more arbitrarily. Because it has been extensively covered in other books, for example, San Francisco has been given relatively shorter shrift here than it truly deserves; and some less famous towns may have been represented beyond what a strictly statistical approach would have allowed.

Besides these conscious decisions, there were also externals that influenced the final selection. Many exceptionally fine houses proved to be practically impossible to photograph because of obstructions like trees and power lines. And during the photographic phase of the project a few sumptuous examples chanced to be undergoing long-term renovation. No doubt, there were others that were simply overlooked in the course of gathering the material.

What remains, then, is a somewhat selective but still (one hopes) representative sampling of some of the more interesting West Coast Victorians bequeathed to us from the last century. As a glance will show, however, many of them are not located anywhere near the ocean, so the term "West Coast" itself needs definition. In the pre-railroad period most of the larger inland settlements in California, Oregon, and Washington were founded on some navigable body of water and were thus, in some extended sense, "coastal" even though not actually located on the Pacific shore itself. As it happens, moreover, the distribution of Victorian architecture in the far West coincides closely with the area's coast and river systems. As used here, then, the term "West Coast" includes not only the rather narrow plain bounded by the coast ranges, but also the river valley systems that extend eastward to the Sierras and Cascades.

In an age when river travel has become little more than a quaint memory it is easy to forget the important role it played in the development of communities of every size in the 19th century. Even towns founded by overland pioneers tended to be built on or near navigable waters. In the 1860s it would have been posible (if anyone wanted to do it) to travel from, say, Albany, Oregon to Red Bluff, California entirely by boat. Gold towns, which had an economic *raison d'etre* all their own, might be (and usually were) located inland, as were a number of small communities that sprang up on the main overland routes connecting larger cities. And after the arrival of the railroad other more or less land-locked areas became the sites of new settlements. All this notwithstanding, the fact remains that the majority of West Coast towns and cities founded in the 19th century were located either on the coast or near bodies of water linked to it and were thus connected to the established cultural centers of the eastern seaboard.

This had a direct effect on the region's architecture. The coast and its river extensions were instrumental in helping Victorian architecture establish itself in settlements throughout the area. And though certain localities tended to favor particular styles and idioms, a measure of homogeneity existed from northern to southern border. Italianate house types that first became popular in San Francisco, for instance, soon appeared in such diverse towns as San Diego, Astoria, Portland, and Seattle, and the later Eastlake and Queen Anne Styles also spread with amazing rapidity. After the arrival of the railroad, Victorians became commonplace even in the hinterlands.

Is there, then, an identifiable West Coast strain of Victorian architecture? Not quite—though building in the region did take some idiosyncratic turns. By the 1880s a distinctive blend of Italianate, Stick, and Eastlake elements had become recognizable as the "San Francisco Style," and because of the extensive and elaborate use to which it was put there, the bay window also became firmly identified with the architecture of the city. In parts of the Northwest, moreover, there were preferences for and adaptations of particular stylistic modes. Downingesque forms enjoyed considerable popularity in Oregon, and Italianate houses sometimes acquired uncharacteristically steep roofs. Notwithstanding these local and regional proclivities, however, Victorian architecture on the West Coast derived in the main from styles borrowed from the East.

This influence was especially apparent in the earliest years of American settlement on the Pacific. The first of the styles we now call Victorian—the Gothic Revival—was initially carried to California from New England in the form of prefabricated houses. These began arriving in 1849 or thereabouts, and some examples date from as late as 1860. In addition, pattern books, almost all of which were published in the East, also played a significant role in transmitting the vocabulary of styles that had achieved currency on the Atlantic seaboard. In the first decades after the gold rush the works of Andrew Jackson Downing were quite influential, particularly his *Architecture of Country Houses* (1850). And toward the end of the century the various books of a mail-order architect, George Franklin Barber, seem to have enjoyed considerable popularity.

As might be expected, something of a cultural lag existed between East and West. It generally took the better part of a decade for architectural styles to reach the West Coast, and they continued to find employment there long after they were out of fashion on the Atlantic. This stylistic gap was, of course, less apparent in larger cities and most pronounced in rural areas, where, for example, Gothic and Italianate houses were still being built as late as the 1880s and 90s. Though it diminished as the century wore on, particularly after the coming of the steel rail, the discrepancy never disappeared entirely during the Victorian era.

On the West Coast, San Francisco was the most important source of architectural ideas. As the most populous city west of the Rockies it was also the most influential and imitated. In the first decades following the gold rush, eastern styles were commonly transmitted to other West Coast cities via the Golden Gate, and it was not long before the new western capital began to emerge as a fount of inspiration in its own right. Trained architects had begun arriving as early as the 1850s, and within a few decades they were helping San Francisco forge its own characteristic architectural style.

Much of the regional hegemony the city enjoyed had an economic basis. In Southern California and the Northwest entire communities were built on supplying San Francisco with its various needs and desires—lumber, beef, butter, oysters—and this commercial traffic naturally led to architectural borrowing. When a northern lumber baron or shipping magnate decided to build a proper mansion, the great houses of San Francisco were generally the models, and, as likely as not, it would be a San Francisco architect who was commissioned to do the job. The local landmarks that resulted in turn helped to disseminate architectural ideas by providing inspiration for a host of lesser dwellings.

Lumber also played a significant role in the development of architecture on the West Coast. It was important in most of the rest of the country too, of course: in the 19th century, as in our own, the majority of houses in the United States were constructed of this readily available, eminently workable material. But on the Pacific Coast its dominance over brick and stone was nearly complete. It has been estimated that nine-tenths of the houses erected in San Francisco in the Victorian era were built of wood—a percentage that easily holds true for the region as a whole.

This overwhelming preference was partially due to the ready availability of vast stands of timber in Northern California, Oregon, and Washington. However, in San Francisco and other parts of California, another factor was a fear of earthquakes, which, understandably, discouraged the use of rigid building materials. Moreover, the ingredients needed to make brick were in short supply in many communities, and the means to transport stone from inland quarries were generally lacking. As a result 19th-century domestic architecture on the West Coast is comprised almost entirely of wooden houses. The forms that many of them assumed, moreover, show the influence of some striking developments in carpentry and building that had taken place in the last half of the century.

New ways of working wood affected Victorian design in a number of ways. Much of the characteristic decoration of the age, for instance, stemmed from innovations in millworking. The flat-cut gingerbread of the earliest decorative styles was a direct outcome of the invention of the scroll saw, and toward the end of the century, a host of new steam-powered milling machines gave rise to the cut and turned fancy-work that characterized the later Victorian modes.

However, the most important advance in building technique in the 19th century was the advent of the mass-produced nail and the subsequent development of the "balloon" frame. Before the common wire nail became cheaply and readily available, houses were almost always supported by heavy posts and beams held together with pegs—a technique that traced back to medieval times. The manufactured wire nail changed all this by making the lighter, more adaptable balloon frame possible. Workers using the new system could frame a house in a fraction of the time required by the old, and some of the labor thus saved was inevitably translated into design. Suddenly it became easy for houses to break out of the boxy shapes of the past, to explore freer, more functional plans, and to sprout such typical Victorian extensions as bays and towers.

This boon to construction, which is thought to have developed in the Midwest in the 1830s, had become an established part of the building tradition of the nation by the time the Pacific was opened up to settlement. That a 19th-century trade journal would erroneously identify its origins with the "California Style" only serves to demonstrate how widespread its use had become in the West. The special importance of the balloon frame in the development and dissemination of architectural style was that its use required no special training or skill. This new technique which lent itself so readily to the production of Victorian forms was immediately available to local builders. In addition, the various decorative modes that sprang up at about the same time—essentially just new ways of working wood—were easily imitated by any good workman who had the right tools. The simplicity of wooden construction and decoration thus almost guaranteed the spread of Victorian House Styles in any area where lumber was readily available.

In Northern California, one particular type of lumber, redwood, had a special influence. Its widespread use accounts both for some of the more spectacular examples of Victorian extravagance and for the fact that many of them are still here today. This material proved particularly amenable to ornamental elaboration of all sorts (as witness the William Carson Mansion), and its durability and resistance to rot and decay is almost legendary. Its extensive use in San Francisco, Eureka, and some other communities helps explain the relatively high survival rate of Victoriana in those cities.

In recent years old houses like these have been receiving a lot of attention from various sources: architects, historians, photographers, designers, incurable romantics, and the nostalgia-prone—to name a few. In the midst of all this enthusiasm it is easy to forget that for most of the 20th century Victorian architecture was not so fondly regarded. Until at least the late 1960s the proverbial man on the street tended to see them as fussy and old fashioned—quaint at best; and the opinions of professional tastemakers were often much harsher. Critics cited Victorians as examples of dishonest architecture and deplored them as relics of the robber baron era. The mansions were pilloried as outrageous displays of conspicuous consumption and the cottages derided as pathetic expressions of bourgeois upward-striving. Historians were apt to write off the entire era as a period of lapsed taste in the noble history of architecture. And among architects themselves, Victorian design was generally despised. John W. Root used to refer to the Queen Anne as "The Tubercular Style;" and Frank Lloyd Wright once characterized most of the buildings of the era as "mistakes"—though (with a wink to historical preservation) he allowed that we ought to keep them around anyway to remind ourselves not to make any more like them.

Today, with Victorians more or less back in favor, most of these opinions have been revised and softened. The ornament and general complication once decried as dishonest is now seen as whimsical and romantic. And far from regarding them as "mistakes," recent generations have tended to be delighted with these effusive old structures and the evidence they provide that our allegedly staid ancestors were actually having fun with their architecture—a subject the 20th century treats with the utmost sobriety. As for the robber barons . . . well, all that seems like a Sunday-school picnic from the perspective of the 1980s: one tendency today is to view Victorian houses as quaint reminders of a genteel and gracious past.

The reasons for this renewed interest are various. One of them, certainly, has to do with the heightened historical awareness sparked by the national bicentennial. As the country's two-hundredth birthday drew near, people increasingly began to recognize some of those dowdy old houses down the block as genuine nuggets of Americana and often became involved in restoring and preserving them. Historical societies and civic groups pooled their resources to refurbish local landmarks gone to seed. And long-time Victorian owners struggled with the paperwork and documentation needed to get their homes listed on the National Register.

Economic incentives also helped rekindle an interest in the architecture of the period. For a while at least, some would-be home-owners were drawn into the old-house game by promises of tax and loan benefits. But even without these positive inducements, which are now largely a thing of the past, restoring an existing house, rather than building a new one, often made a lot of sense in the real estate markets of the 1970s and 80s. Moreover, the philosophy of restoration dovetailed neatly with several of the economic gospels that have enjoyed recent popularity. For some homeowners "no growth" and "less is more" came to mean a Volvo parked in front of an immaculately restored 19th-century cottage. Victorians have also been caught up in the recycling movement. It is now common, even trendy, for lawyers, accountants, and doctors to work out of spruced-up 19th century houses. And their wholesale conversion to bed and breakfasts is a phenomenon in its own right.

Meanwhile, it seems, these survivors are even beginning to be taken seriously as architecture. The later eclectic styles, for instance, have been celebrated as the first uniquely American contributions to the art and science of building. And some historians have seen the unprece-dented new freedom of plan that characterized many 19th-century houses as an early manifestation of "organic" architecture. Still others insist that in their exuberance and complication Victorians address psychological needs that modern forms ignore entirely.

This last idea suggests another reason for the rebirth of interest in Victorian design. With its emphasis on clean lines and hard-edged geometry, modern architecture has often seemed a bit cold to many who grew up in its spare embrace; and to those who harbor a touch of the romantic or who have concluded—like the author of a recurrent line of graffiti—that "less is a bore," the profusion of elements in a Victorian house can be well nigh irresistible.

As a whole, Victorian architecture was an expression of 19th-century romanticism. The earliest revival styles were attempts to identify with an idealized pre-industrial past. It is not coincidental that they occurred just as industrialization and modern transportation were sweeping the old values away forever, nor that they persisted longest in relatively remote rural areas. The later eclectic styles of the era, however, reflect the romantic spirit in a somewhat different incarnation. This was the romance of rugged individualism, of men who gloried in their mastery over nature and her materials and who reveled in the technological powers that the genie of the new age had bestowed upon them. In the last decades of the 19th century the overall feeling was one of bold self-confidence. In contrast to the austerity of modern architecture, the temperament of the late Victorian era was expressed in buildings that actively courted formal complexity and extravagant ornament. They were monuments to the self-assurance of the age. Today these millionaires' mansions may seem embarrassing in their frank revelation of their owner's overweening pride, but in their own day they were more than this. They were also genuine, if naive expressions of a basic faith in the community, the nation, the times themselves. These were the days (we have to remind ourselves) when businessmen still unblushingly described themselves as capitalists, and when the schism between the public and the private good did not seem to yawn as widely as it does today.

Much of this optimism, of course, has not been borne-out by subsequent history. It has been left to future generations to try to coax the recalcitrant genie of industrialization back into his bottle. It is ironic that where progress has reigned unchecked the most sumptuous products of the Victorian era have largely disappeared: most of those that have survived to the present have done so precisely because their communities failed to develop beyond the end of the century. Like the diners and filling stations on old Route 66, many of them are still around only because the freeway to progress was built elsewhere. Two cities on Puget Sound offer convenient examples: Seattle, now the largest city in the Northwest, is conspicuous for its lack of 19th-century domestic architecture, while Port Townsend, which failed in its final bid for regional ascendency in the 1890s, is filled with it. San Francisco remains the single, somewhat perplexing exception to the rule that the larger the city, the less likely it is to have maintained a significant Victorian presence.

For the time being at least the general rescue of American's 19th-century heritage that began a couple of decades ago seems to be proceeding apace. Though many Victorians were razed during the years when they were decidedly out of fashion, enough of them have survived in smaller out-of-the-way locations to satisfy at least part of the current passion for them. And most of those that are still with us today are being carefully tended. This phenomenon is a national one, but is particularly apparent on the West Coast in towns like Port Townsend in Washington, Albany in Oregon, and Eureka in California—all of which have scores of 19th-century houses in various stages of restoration.

All the patching and painting that has been going on recently has generally been good both for individual homeowners and their communities. City planners have discovered that restoration programs—official and otherwise—are remarkably effective in upgrading marginal neighborhoods; and civic leaders have credited the new interest in Victoriana with generating enhanced community pride and cohesion—not to mention tax and tourist dollars. As for those venturesome souls who have mustered the time, money and energy required to restore a decrepit, hundred-year-old manse to pristinity, the rewards should be self-evident: a handsome place to live, a little piece of history, and the satisfactions of a job well done.

For the rest of us, the benefits may be less tangible, but no less significant. On a simple visual level the streets (some of them at least) are more interesting to look at these days: there is more out there to catch and fascinate the eye. But beyond this, these survivors from the Victorian past have a lot to tell us—and not just about relatively minor changes in architectural fashion. They also speak volumes about social values, economic rhythms, and the organic life of cities and entire regions. Even more important, perhaps, these old mansions and cottages are among the most concrete links we have with our own history. And it may be in this—their power to evoke time passed and establish its continuity with the present—that the Victorians have their greatest claim on our attention.

FRISBIE-WALSH HOUSE c.1850: Benicia, California

Prefabrication was a partial solution to the housing shortage that developed when thousands of gold seekers and camp followers began pouring through San Francisco on their way to the mother-lode country in 1849. While local building industries were mustering themselves, hundreds of prebuilt structures were brought into California by ship. Some of these are reported to have come from as far away as Europe and China, but most originated in New England where the Gothic Revival was at the height of its popularity. As a result, the first of the styles we now call "Victorian" was literally shipped to the West Coast.

The house shown here is thought to be one of three identical Gothic Revival cottages constructed in Boston, brought 'round the horn in sections, and assembled in California. Of the other two, one was erected in San Francisco and later destroyed, while the second, the General Vallejo Residence in nearby Sonoma, is still standing today. The Benicia house appears to have been built—or at least assembled—for John Frisbie, a banker and landowner who married Epifania de Guadalupe Vallejo, the daughter of the aforementioned general. However it was soon acquired by John Walsh, a sea captain from Nova Scotia, who settled in the area in 1849 or '50 to take a job as customs collector.

In style the Frisbie-Walsh House is almost pure Carpenter's Gothic. Its steep-pitched roof, distinctive gable ornament, and pointed windows are the most overtly typical features of the style; but the asymmetrical floor plan, one-story porch, and dormer windows are characteristic as well. The horizontal siding seen here was also common, though some 19th-century tastemakers considered vertical board and batten more appropriate for houses in "the pointed style."

FORT DALLES SURGEON'S QUARTERS 1857: The Dalles, Oregon

Figure 1: from *The Architecture of Country Houses*

In the Northwest, as in much of the rest of America in the mid-1800s, professional and nonprofessional builders alike relied heavily on books for practical, aesthetic, and even moral advice on architecture. The various works of Andrew Jackson Downing were particularly popular in the early Victorian period and had an enormous influence on building throughout the country. One persistent ideal in his writings, "tasteful simplicity," is exemplified in the house shown here.

Built at Fort Dalles, where the Oregon trail meets the Columbia River, the Surgeon's Quarters is based on a design for "A Symmetrical Bracketed Cottage" (fig. 1) reproduced in Downing's *Architecture of Country Houses* (1850). As the author pointed out, the rather basic plan is enhanced by some simple but effective details: the gable that projects over the small porch, the hooded and bracketed windows, the vertical board and batten siding. All in all he wrote:

> *No person would build such a quaint yet modest porch as this, no one would give this simple character of beauty to the windows, and no one would reach this exact height of tasteful simplicity in the whole exterior character, unless he had a real appreciation of the beautiful and truthful in cottage life....*

This was not merely aesthetics: for Downing "the beautiful and truthful" made architecture a powerful instrument for promoting civilization. "So long as men are forced to dwell in log huts and follow a hunter's life," he counseled:

> *we must not be surprised at lynch law and the use of the bowie knife. But when smiling lawns and tasteful cottages begin to embellish a country, we know that order and culture are established.*

Perhaps Captain Thomas Jordan, the officer in charge of construction at Fort Dalles, and Louis Scholl, the German draftsman who adapted the plans from Downing's book, had these thoughts in mind when they built this "tasteful cottage" at a site where every new settler coming into the region by the overland route would be sure to see it. Then again, perhaps they only wanted to add a touch of style to a dreary frontier outpost. In any event the cottage was only one of a number of Downingesque designs they employed during the enlargement of the fort occasioned by the Yakima Indian War of 1855–58.

The army, however, seemed to lack "a real appreciation of the beautiful and truthful in cottage life." Scholl and Jordan received some criticism for their efforts, and soon after an inspection of the new buildings by the commanding general in the area, a directive was issued ordering all future army construction to be "of the plainest kind." The Surgeon's Quarters, an almost unique remnant of "picturesque" military architecture, now serves as a museum.

23

CROSBY HOUSE c.1858: Tumwater, Washington

This house was built by the Crosby clan which came—twenty four family members in all—from Maine to the Tumwater Falls area in 1849. The wood for its construction was probably supplied by Clanrick Crosby who ran the family mill, but it was first occupied by Nathanial and Cordelia, who, as it happen, were Bing Crosby's grandparents. In style the house is primarily Gothic Revival as evidenced by the steep pitch of both the main and dormer roofs and the wavy-line verge board. This latter feature, however, is thought to have been added in the 1880s. The front-gabled arrangement is relatively rare for Gothic houses on the West Coast, and this (along with the side and transom lights at the front entrance) suggests the influence of the earlier Greek Revival. The house is now maintained jointly by the city of Tumwater and the Daughters of the Pioneers of Washington. Pending repairs it will be open to the public for tours.

BENJAMIN LATHROP HOUSE 1860: Redwood City, California

As its name implies, Redwood City was once a lumber center. Its proximity to San Francisco, however, made it one of the first areas on the West Coast to be completely deforested. It was settled in the early 1850s, but within a decade or so the only reminder of the huge trees that once covered the area was the name of the town. Most of its early architecture has also disappeared, and this house is one of the few survivors from the 19th century that remains. It was originally the residence of Benjamin Lathrop, an early settler in the community. Recently restored and adapted for commercial use, it stands today essentially as it was when it was first built: a two-story Gothic Revival cottage with characteristic gable decoration.

B. F. DOWELL HOUSE 1861: Jacksonville, Oregon

For the West, and especially for an Oregon gold-mining town, the B. F. Dowell House is a remarkably early example of the Italianate Style that flourished in America from the 1850s to the 1880s. The prototypes for houses like this one were vernacular Italian forms popularized on this side of the Atlantic by A. J. Downing and others. Broadly they were of two types: rambling, "picturesque" villas, and more formal, symmetrical dwellings which were usually designated as "Tuscan."

The Dowell residence, which falls into the latter category, illustrates one way that architectural styles evolved in the 19th century. The rectangular box form for houses could be given any number of "looks"—Greek, Italian, even Egyptian—by the addition or subtraction of a few stylistic details. Here the basic box is Tuscan by virtue of its round-headed windows, classical portico, and frontal symmetry. Its low-pitched, hipped roof is also typical, though in this case it is actually a replacement for a flat one that originally capped the structure. Except for the absence of ornamental brackets beneath the eaves and, perhaps, a cupola, the Dowell House might have been lifted right out of the pages of one of A. J. Downing's books. Certainly its brick construction—rare in Oregon before the turn of the century, and almost unprecedented in gold-mining towns—would have found favor with that arbiter of early Victorian taste. Downing liked buildings to endure. "We greatly prefer a cottage of brick or rough stone," he wrote in 1850, "to one of wood."

Benjamin Franklin Dowell (named for his more famous ancestor) was not a gold miner, incidentally, but a lawyer. Schooled in Virginia, he came to Oregon on the heels of the gold strike that gave birth to Jacksonville in 1851 and, like Leland Stanford in California (pp. 30–31), made his living trading with the miners for several years. By the time his brick house was ready for occupancy, however, the gold was already beginning to play out and Dowell had resumed the practice of law.

STANFORD-LATHROP HOUSE c.1861: Sacramento, California

Though originally built in the 1850s as a two-story residence in the Georgian mode, this house was later enlarged and altered to reflect the newer Italianate and Second Empire Styles. The initial design is credited to Seth Babson, an architect who came to California from New England in 1850, but it is not clear whether he was also responsible for the remodeling. First owned by a wholesale merchant, Sheldon C. Fogus, the house was purchased by Leland Stanford in 1861 and served as the California gubernatorial mansion during his term in office. Soon after he acquired it, Stanford had the basement raised and added a mansard roof to create a four-story house. The exterior has remained substantially unchanged since these alternations in the early 1860s.

In that period the Second Empire Style was relatively new even in the East; so its appearance on the West Coast at such an early date is remarkable. Besides the distinctive roof, the residence exhibits several other features that often went along with the mansard: the roof dormers, molded cornices, decorative brackets, hooded windows, and symmetrical facade are all typical. Most of these, of course, were also common in Italianate houses: it is the roof that distinguishes this example as a representative of the French Style.

This fashionable architectural mode was often favored by men who were on the rise socially, economically, and in government—all true of Leland Stanford. Trained as a lawyer, he had come west in 1852 and soon established a very successful mercantile operation in the gold country near Placerville. He married Jane Eliza Lathrop in 1855, and a few years later made a successful bid for the governorship. After his term in office he moved his family to Nob Hill in San Francisco where he was associated with such wealthy luminaries as Collin P. Huntington, Charles Crocker, and Mark Hopkins. Eventually he became the first president of the Central Pacific Railroad and was later elected to the U.S. Senate. Stanford University in Palo Alto is named in memory of his son, Leland Junior, who contracted a fatal illness while travelling in Europe.

SHAW HOUSE c.1866: Ferndale, California

Almost from its beginnings in the 1850s, Ferndale, a small town south of Eureka, prospered as a dairy center. By the late 1870s there was regular steamship service between nearby Port Kenyon and San Francisco, and on the southbound run the cargo was mostly butter. In the 1880s and '90s Ferndale was known as "Cream City" and its substantial Italianate and Eastlake residences were called "Butterfat Palaces." The boom period ended early in the 20th century when the Salt River silted up and ceased to be navigable. But by that time water transportation had become less crucial than in the past, so the town went on in relative prosperity.

Its continued reliance on dairy farming as the basis of its economy, its somewhat isolated location, and the early preservation efforts of some of its citizens have all tended to protect the architecture it inherited from the Victorian era. As a result, Ferndale today is an amazingly well-preserved 19th-century village.

The house shown here, the oldest in the community, was built by Seth Shaw, one of the first settlers to arrive in the area in the early 1850s. His homestead, which he called "Fern Dale," served as the first post office in the area and thus provided a ready name for the town that sprang up around it. Though he began building it in 1854, the cottage was not completed in final form until the middle of the next decade. It seems likely that the specifically Gothic elements—steep gables, pointed windows, gingerbread decoration—were applied in the last phase of construction. Without these the result might have been a fairly ordinary clapboard house. The projecting front wing that divides the porch into two parts is an unusual modification of the more common central-gabled plan often seen in Gothic cottages. The house is now a bed and breakfast establishment, "The Shaw House Inn."

Figure 2: From *Village and Farm Cottages*

PETERS-WINTERMEIER HOUSE c.1869: Eugene, Oregon

In an attempt to follow up on the success of *The Architecture of Country Houses* after A. J. Downing's untimely death in 1852, his publisher, D. Appleton, turned to the architectural firm of Cleaveland and Backus Brothers for a similar book. The result was a volume titled *Village and Farm Cottages* (1856). In general it followed the formula established by Downing and others: practical advice on building coupled with moral injunction on the need for good architecture. But the new authors limited their book to designs "for an humbler class of structures" than Downing's, and addressed themselves to a specific audience, one they described as:

> *a class, numerous and important in every community . . . comprehending mechanics and tradesmen of moderate circumstances, the small farmer, and the laboring man generally.*

To this group, the architects' message was a simple one: escape the city and "the evils of tenant life," move to the country and build a home of your own. To encourage and provide for the expected exodus, Cleaveland and Backus brothers included twenty-four designs for economical dwellings "beyond the reach of no capable and industrious man."

Though no information has survived on who built the house shown here, it is clearly based on Design No. 12 (fig. 2) in their book, which was reprinted in 1869. First owned by A. V. Peters, a French immigrant who ran a general store in Eugene City, it is a particularly fine example in the Rural Gothic or Downingesque Cottage mode. As illustrated in this example, the distinguishing features of the style include a steep-pitched roof, decorative brackets under the eaves, and vertical board and batten siding. The house departs from the published design in some respects: the bay window on the projecting wing is not included in the rendering, and there are some differences in porch and window details; but in general it closely approximates the plan that appears in the book.

It is anyone's guess whether the builder drew up his own working drawings or obtained them from the architects, but it is worth mentioning that both editions of *Village and Farm Cottages* advised readers that the printed plans and specifications for this house were available for only $4.00 postpaid.

TOM CRELLIN HOUSE 1869: Oysterville, Washington

Oysterville's economic basis was a small but flavorful shellfish that bred bountifully in the protected waters of the Willapa Bay on the southern coast of Washington. Robert Espy and Isaac Clark, the first white men to settle there permanently, had been guided to the teeming beds by a friendly, but perhaps naive Indian in the early 1850s. Realizing the potential of the area they immediately staked out claims, and the town grew up around them. Never very populous, it nonetheless thrived for twenty-five years or so by trying valiantly to satisfy San Francisco's seemingly insatiable craving for bivalve mollusks. Later in the century, however, its virtual monopoly on the West Coast oyster trade was broken when rival areas were seeded with transplanted eastern shellfish. From that point on the town began to drift into quiet dormancy. It never died completely, but it slept soundly through most of the 20th century. As a result much of its early architecture has survived unscathed by progress.

The cottage shown here was built by Tom Crellin, a pioneer oysterman, originally from the Isle of Man, who came to Washington in the 1850s. Its basic plan is rather similar to the Peters-Wintermeier House (pp. 34–35), except that it rises a full two stories and has a balcony above the porch. Like the residence in Eugene, the one in Oysterville may have been inspired by a pattern book. There are just enough stylistic touches to suggest that it was not the work of an unaided vernacular builder. Note, for example, the flat-cut gingerbread trim on the gables, the hood mold over the second-story window, and the polygonal bay on the projecting wing. The front of the house, incidentally, is not oriented toward the street but toward the water: the direction that probably had the most urgent claim on its owner's attention.

JACOB KAMM HOUSE 1871: Portland, Oregon

Of the various architectural styles popular in America in the Victorian period, the French Second Empire was a particular favorite of the burgeoning upper middle class. Unlike the others it was not a revival style but a contemporary architectural movement. Born in France, the aura of modernity and continental elegance it radiated appealed to those whose tastes—or pretentions—required more sophistication than offered by the Gothic or Italian modes. Its less elegant soubriquet, "The General Grant Style" derived from its frequent use in government buildings during the administration of the 18th president.

The Kamm House is one of the best surviving examples of the style in the Northwest. Most sources agree that it was constructed by the builder L. Therkelsen, and it seems to have been designed by an architect named Justen Krumbein. Besides the mansard roof, it has several other characteristic Second-Empire features: narrow, segmentally arched windows with hoods, round-topped dormers, paired entry doors, and a belt course that serves to indicate on the outside, the division of stories within the house. Though it doesn't look like it, the siding is actually wood—smoothly fitted, painted, and embellished with decorative quoins at the corners to simulate the masonry construction of its prototypes.

Jacob Kamm, for whom the house was built, was one of those fabulous 19th-century figures who combined seemingly unlimited energy with a midas touch. He was born in Switzerland in 1823 but was raised in St. Louis where he became a cabin boy on a Mississippi riverboat and studied marine technology with the Engineers' Association of Missouri. The gold rush years found him in California piloting steamboats on the Sacramento and Feather rivers, and a few years later he was in Portland where he built Oregon's first stern-wheeler, the Jennie Clark. Over a period of time he became a principle stockholder in at least four river transportation companies in the Northwest and—as the railroad began to supplant the steamboat—an equal number of banks. When he died at age 89 he was a wealthy man with his own block of buildings in Portland and a thirteen-acre estate just outside town. Moved to its present location in 1951, Kamm's elegant house was restored by Eric Ladd, a preservation-minded restaurateur. More recently it has been converted for use as an office building.

A. C. PALMER HOUSE 1874: Calistoga, California

Located a bit north of Napa, Calistoga is the site of a natural hot springs, and it was initially promoted as a resort for the well-to-do. Some of its architecture from this early period suggests that these efforts were at least partially successful. The residence pictured here is one of several surviving examples in the elegant French Mansard Style that was evidently popular in the town in the 1870s. It was built by Augustus C. Palmer, Calistoga's first judge and the owner of a large lumber yard in the area. Palmer is reported to have visited Paris in 1870, and this may have inspired him to build in the new French mode; but his house is closer to American variations than to Gallic orginals.

Similar designs were common in the United States in this period. The supplement to *Bicknell's Village Builder* (1872), for instance, contained several "Residences in the French Style" that are essentially the same as the Palmer House. As in this example the basic plan was a rather formal two-story box topped with a mansard roof. The latter feature was considered practical as well as stylish since it effectively provided almost as much space as a third floor. Most of the ornamental details associated with the French mode were like those found in Italianate houses, but with some differences: the modillions beneath the cornice line, for instance, were apt to be smaller and lighter than heavier Italian brackets, and the porch posts and bracings generally showed similar refinement. Another common feature, the full-width porch, was a characteristically American adaptation of the smaller, classically-detailed portico that fronted more traditional representatives of the style—an instance of continental elegance transformed by New World informality.

REED-LYFORD HOUSE c.1874: Tiburon, California

The Reed-Lyford house, an interesting blend of styles, was the home of Dr. Benjamin Lyford—a San Francisco physician turned dairy farmer—and his wife, Hilarita—daughter of John Reed, a wealthy landowner in Marin County. A few years after their marriage in 1872 they moved into the quaint, towered house shown here and established their Eagle Dairy on a portion of an old Spanish land grant, The *Rancho Corte Madera del Presidio,* that Mrs. Lyford's father had acquired before the gold rush. There they led a romantically pastoral life, and, as part of a program to produce milk of superior quality, tended their cows with "great kindness" and extreme attention to hygiene. They also tried to start a sort of utopian, health-minded community on their extensive property and even sold a few lots to selected buyers. But some of the rules—no smoking, drinking, or kissing—were perhaps too strict for popular consumption, and the planned development (named "Lyford Hygeiia" for the doctor and the Greek goddess of health) never attained much success.

No information has survived on who designed their residence, but it is thought to have derived from a pattern book. In style it is mainly Second Empire: both the flared mansard roof and the centrally placed tower are characteristic of houses in the French mode. But the influence of the Italianate is also apparent in the bracketed and pedimented second-floor windows, and there are hints of the Gothic in the pointed gables of the tower dormers. Moreover, the structure has a distinctly churchlike character perhaps appropriate for a man who seems to have made a sort of religion of health.

Moved to its present location and restored by the architect John Lord King in 1957, the former residence now serves as headquarters for the Marin chapter of the National Audubon Society.

POINT FERMIN LIGHTHOUSE 1874: San Pedro, California

Most lighthouses are decidedly functional: when they contain them at all, stylistic references are usually minimal. Point Fermin Light, however, is an exception. Some of its details clearly show the influence of the Stick Style that was popular from the 1870s until it was eclipsed by the newer Eastlake and Queen Anne modes later in the century. Nonetheless, this would be a rather plain house except for the extraordinary, bracketed beacon tower that sprouts from its roof. This unusual addition conjures up some of the romance that has become attached over the years to lighthouses and the solitary men who kept them.

Actually though, it was two *women,* the Smith sisters, who first tended this light—though not for very long. The sentinel had been constructed to warn approaching ships of the rocky hazards just north of the entrance to San Pedro Harbor, and it was built on a lonely promontory several miles from town. San Pedro itself was hardly more than a fishing village in the mid 1870s, and the sisters are said to have resigned out of loneliness after a few months of solitude.

Though it was deactivated after World War II the house was preserved and maintained by a group called The Sons and Daughters of the Golden West. For a time an observation tower covered the lantern housing, but this has been removed, and the structure now stands essentially as it was built—a lighthouse with a unique Victorian touch. It is now a part of Point Fermin Park where it is accessible to the public but not normally open for tours.

ITALIANATE TOWN HOUSE
c.1883: San Francisco, California

Though the pristine dwelling shown here seems actually to have been built in the early 1880s, it exemplifies a stage in the evolution of the town house that is more commonly associated with the two preceding decades. Flat-front, flat-roofed, Italianate boxes like this one were the starting point from which more sophisticated town houses derived in San Francisco. From such basic models they mutated into new shapes, acquired the latest decorative touches, and (along with the closely related rowhouse) multiplied until they became a characteristic part of the city's Victorian architecture.

The Sloss, Vollmer, and Queen Anne Town houses (pp. 47, 84–85, 215) illustrate various stages in this evolution. As it usually occurred the paired windows on the first and second floors would push out into a two-story bay to form a sort of abbreviated ell. The hooded entryway, meanwhile, developed into a small porch or portico often topped with a balcony. Vertical stick-work might rise from the windows to meet the cornice brackets, and Eastlake ornament was likely to appear. At the top of the structure the false front might take on gabled or mansardic disguises, but the actual roof usually remained flat.

Except that its first owner was named Charles White, little is known about the origins of this particular example. Even its year of construction is only approximate since it is based on water department records: city documents that might have dated it precisely were lost in the earthquake and fire of 1906. The house illustrates the danger of dating a building on the basis of style alone, but it is also deceptive in another way—it is actually three stories high. The true ground floor, built on the side of a hill, is practically invisible from street level.

SLOSS HOUSE
1876: San Francisco, California

Built for a businessman named Louis Sloss, this town house illustrates some of the changes that gradually overtook more basic Italianate houses like the one shown on p. 46. In this typical but finely detailed example, the flat front has given way to the bay front. A two story bay window has been added at one side of the facade to give the interior more space and light; and—as if to balance the composition—the entryway is now graced with a portico whose classical columns support a small second-story balcony. Decorative details are still Italianate but are more lavish than in earlier models. Simple corner boards have been replaced with overlapping quoins, and the cornice brackets have multiplied and grown more complex. Aside from their overall proportions, what remain essentially the same in both town houses are the segmentally arched windows and the bracketed pediments that crown them.

Though bay-front Italianate town houses like this one attained their greatest popularity in San Francisco, variations on the theme occurred in other towns up and down the coast. Outside the Bay Area, there are surviving examples in Portland and Astoria, but in most other cities they have fallen victim to progress.

ANTHONY HOUSE c.1876: Alameda, California

By the early 1860s Alameda had already established an identity as one of the more fashionable suburban communities on the east side of the San Francisco bay. In 1869 its growth was augmented when it became the western terminus of the transcontinental railway. Since the town is more or less surrounded by water, however, expansion could not go on indefinitely, and some of its houses seem to have been designed with this awareness. For psychological as well as practical reasons, perhaps, many of them were built more like city houses than suburban ones. The residence shown here, for instance, looks like a town house from the front. To the rear it breaks into bays and wings (and out of the rectangular shape that confined most similar forms in the city), but to the street it presents the same bay-front facade that had become a typical sight in San Francisco by the late 1870s.

The house was originally the residence of John Anthony, a railroad official, and is probably the finest representative of the Italianate Style remaining in the city. In many respects it is similar to the Sloss House (p. 47), but some of its ornamental details—the incised designs in the portico, the rosettes that crown the window surrounds—are quite extraordinary.

CAMRON-STANFORD HOUSE 1876: Oakland, California

In the suburbs and country, the Italianate house usually assumed a more horizontal configuration than in the city. The less restricted space provided greater freedom for the rambling, irregular shapes of the prototypical Italian farmhouses idealized by adherants of "the picturesque." Some of this is apparent in the Camron-Stanford House which has added wings, bays, and an off-center entry to the basic cube. In ornamental details, however, it is quite similar to the town houses illustrated on the last several pages. The flat roof, brackets, and rounded windows were typical of the style in all its variants. The lower windows, by the way, are full arched or round headed; the upper ones display the segmental arch.

This house is the last of a number of opulent Victorians that once populated Oakland's Lake Merritt district. It was originally owned by Will and Alice Camron, he a young man who seems to have been something of a cowboy, she the heiress to a fortune her father, John Marsh, had acquired in the cattle business. Except for her inheritance, however, Alice Marsh seems to have been born for bad luck: her mother died shortly after her birth, her father was ambushed and killed by outlaws some years later, and her young daughter died of food poisoning not long after the family took up residence in this house. The Camrons subsequently put the property up for sale, and it was eventually purchased by Josiah Stanford, Leland Stanford's brother. Later, in the 20th century, the City of Oakland acquired it for use as a museum. Threatened with demolition in the early 1970s, it was rescued and restored by preservationists who recognized its historical and architectural value. It is now open to the public for tours.

ISAAC WOOLEN HOUSE 1876: Ashland, Oregon

Perhaps because Ashland lay on the main route between Portland and Sacramento, the fashionable Italianate Style was quickly adopted for some of the more imposing residences in town. Some of these followed big-city patterns rather closely, but others—like the one pictured here—show some interesting departures from the norm. In deference to the climate, Italianate variants in the Northwest were sometimes capped with steeper roofs than the flat or low-angled ones usually associated with the style. This adaptation, also seen in the Laughlin and Keyes residences, (pp. 56–59, 190–191) is particularly evident in the Isaac Woolen house.

This was originally the home of a successful farmer from the Bear Creek Valley who, after remarrying at the age of 54, left his farm and established a residence in town. Except for the steep-pitched roof most of its features are distinctly Italianate. The ornate brackets, hooded, segmentally arched windows, and classical portico are among the defining characteristics of the style. The asymmetrical facade, polygonal and rectangular bays, and horizontal siding were also common. No records indicate who was responsible for the actual construction, but this and several other Italianate houses in town indicate that at least one fine craftsman was working in Ashland in the 1870s and 80s. The Woolen House is especially interesting in comparison to its next-door neighbor, the W. H. Atkinson residence (p. 64–65) which has some similar decorative features but is very different in overall configuration.

52

MCDONALD HOUSE 1878: Santa Rosa, California

This Northern California mansion was built by Mark Lindsay McDonald, an honorary Kentucky Colonel, who came to Santa Rosa in 1869 to deal in land but stayed on to became a permanent resident. Born of an old Virginia family, he had come west as the captain of a wagon train in the 1850s and made his initial stake as a road engineer for the Virginia City silver mines. He later acquired a comfortable fortune on the San Francisco stock market and—still later—came to Santa Rosa where he subdivided what became known as the McDonald Addition and started his own fruit packing company. He also helped establish the city water works, created the municipal street car system (horse-drawn in that early period) and was instrumental through his connections with Leland Stanford in bringing the railroad to town. In addition, he served on the city council, where, one may assume, he had a considerable influence in local government.

"Mableton," as this house was originally known, remains the premier residence in the neighborhood McDonald developed. From a formal standpoint it is an expansive, symmetrically arranged, two-story, raised-basement house with a modified hipped roof and a broad verandah surrounding it on three sides. From the point of view of *style,* however, it is less easy to categorize. It has been described variously as exhibiting Stick, Gothic, and "Southern" features—all of which may be true. But the simpler truth may be that the design is either so individual or so eclectic that it has no obvious precedents or imitators. Unfortunately, neither the architect nor the builder have been identified.

LEE LAUGHLIN HOUSE 1879: Yamhill, Oregon

When this house was built, Lee Laughlin was a state senator and businessman with the usual investments in real estate, banking, and politics. In his youth, however, he led a wilder life. He had come to Oregon from Missouri with his parents in 1847, but two years later set off on his own for the California gold fields. He was then 16 years old. Returning to Yamhill a few years later he homesteaded briefly but then enlisted to fight in the Yakima Indian war of 1855. Whether or not he saw the Downingesque cottages Louis Scholl was building at Fort Dalles (pp. 22-23) at the end of that campaign is a matter for speculation.

Who designed his residence is also lost to history, but it is notable as a particularly fine example in the Gothic Revival mode. In addition it illustrates, more pointedly than most other examples is this book, a blending of styles typical of the period. The second story with its bargeboards, pointed windows, and steep gables is distinctly Gothic, while the first floor has a number of details—bays, decorative brackets, and horizontal shiplap siding—that are more commonly associated with houses in the Italian manner. Though nominally distinct, elements of these two styles were commonly mixed in both the literature and the actual building practice of the period—particularly in rural areas, where the shade of A. J. Downing lingered on long after his death.

BISHOP'S HOUSE 1879: Portland, Oregon

Perhaps because influential writers like A. J. Downing had stressed the particular suitability of the Gothic Revival Style for country living, it was never widely adopted for housing in the city. The Bishop's House in Portland is an exception to the rule: here the style has taken on urban trappings. Though it has little in common with the picturesque cottages Downing advocated, it is Gothic nevertheless in its allusions to the church architecture of its own century and, beyond that, to the medieval cathedrals of Europe. The overhanging roofs and asymmetrical configurations of its country cousins have necessarily been abandoned, but Gothic styling is still apparent in the pointed arches and tracery of the third-floor windows and in the steep-pitched false gable that rises above the roofline. In addition, the design—attributed to a San Francisco architect named P. Heurn—exploits its narrow city lot to achieve the upward soaring feeling that virtually defines Gothic architecture.

This "High Victorian" phase of the style, which owed much to the influence of the English writer John Ruskin, was more commonly found in churches and public buildings than in domestic architecture. Even though the Bishop's House was originally built to serve as the living quarters of a local prelate, it is more a church annex than a house. After the cathedral next door was destroyed in 1890, the structure was adapted for use as office and commercial space—it is said to have been a speakeasy during prohibition—and was apparently never again used as a residence.

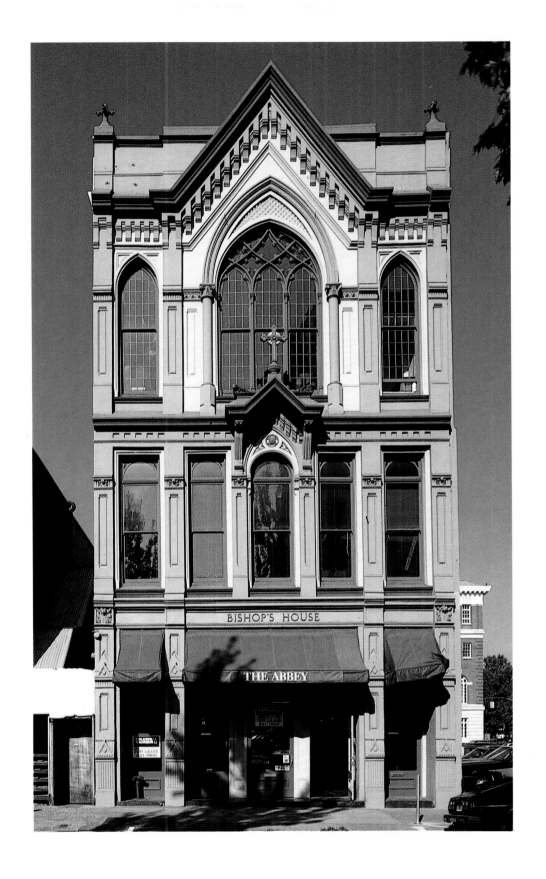

BISHOP'S HOUSE

THE ABBEY

C. H. PAGE HOUSE, c.1879: Astoria, Oregon

Although founded as a fur trading outpost in 1811, Astoria did not really begin to develop as a permanent settlement until after the arrival of the first wagon trains in the 1840s. When this house was built thirty years later, the town was thriving. Its location at the mouth of the Columbia midway between Puget Sound and San Francisco was very favorable for its shipping, logging, and salmon canning activities.

The Page House, one of Astoria's earliest examples in the Italianate Style, is similar to the bay-front town houses popular in San Francisco in the same period. Besides the characteristic facade, it displays the Italianate detailing usual in such houses and has the same flat roof and sidewise orientation to the street.

Local tradition has it that the residence was a wedding gift from Captain Hiram Brown, a Columbia River pilot, to his daughter, Annie, and her husband, C. H. Page, who happened to be one of Brown's business partners. For a time it was known as the *Judge* Page House, but that single title scarcely does justice to the range of the man's activities. In the period from 1875 to 1900 he served successively as a storekeeper, lawyer, city council member, city attorney, county judge, mayor, bank president, and port customs collector. He also helped organize the local gaslight company as well as the Columbia River Railway. All too much, perhaps, for Mrs Page: they were divorced in 1896.

61

63

ATKINSON HOUSE 1880: Ashland, Oregon

This house with its lacy filagree was the home of William H. Atkinson, an Englishman by birth, who grew up in the Midwest and came to Oregon in 1874. After establishing financial interests in the local flour and wool industries, and before going on to become one of the founders and first president of the Bank of Ashland, he paused briefly to build this residence in the Italianate mode favored by many of the town's leading citizens. It is particularly noteworthy for the wooden fancywork that embellishes its porch, balcony, and eaves. The scroll-brackets with decorative pendants are similar, but not identical to those of the Isaac Woolen House next door (pp. 52-53). The jig-cut porch railing is original, but the second floor balustrade may be a replacement. A tidy example of Americanized Italianate, the house is now a bed and breakfast inn.

KELLY-GRIGGS HOUSE c.1880: Red Bluff, California

Founded in the early 1850s, Red Bluff was propitiously located at the navigable headwaters of the Sacramento River and the foot of the northern trail to Oregon. As a result it developed not only as an agricultural settlement but also as a river, stage, and railroad crossroads. As in other small inland towns on a main route, many of its homes quickly adopted styles that were fashionable in larger cities.

The residence shown here is representative of a type of symmetrical, double-bay Italianate house that was popular in the hinterlands as well as on the coast in the 1870s and 80s. In the city such houses were often arranged as duplexes: in smaller towns and in the suburbs they were more likely to be expansive, single-family dwellings. The relationship of this to other common types should be apparent: block out a third of the facade, and what is left is the bay-front town house that was so popular in San Francisco (p. 46); add wings and a tower, and the villa form starts to emerge; build it on a story-and-a-half plan, and it begins to resemble houses like the W. S. Clark residence in Eureka (pp. 104–105). However, this particular example is not quite typical: its squared bays are somewhat unusual for this relatively early period when polygonal ones were more common.

The house was built by Sidney Allen Griggs, a prosperous sheep rancher in the area, and was later acquired by the Kellys, an Irish family who came to Red Bluff by way of Australia. The former residence is now the Kelly-Griggs House Museum. Staffed and maintained by a local volunteer organization, it has been furnished with antiques and historical collections and is open to the public.

MOYER HOUSE 1881: Brownsville, Oregon

Though construction began in 1878, this Italianate Villa was not completed until three years later. John M. Moyer, who built it, appears to have done much of the work himself and is said to have handpicked the lumber for its construction from his own mill. Moyer had apprenticed as a carpenter in the East and arrived in Oregon in 1852 when he was 23 years old. He quickly found work building houses in the Brownsville area east of the Willamette Valley, but seeking a more lucrative profession he tried his hand at a variety of other callings—farming, cattle driving, and gold mining—before acquiring part ownership in a planning mill in 1863. This seems to have been the turning point in his fortunes, but it may also have helped that he married Elizabeth Brown, the daughter of the town's founder. In any event, he soon held interests in the local bank and woolen mill and was later elected as Brownsville's first mayor.

Eventually he had enough capital to begin constructing this residence in the Italianate Style that was still popular in the West forty years after its first appearance in the East. Moyer is supposed to have drawn up the plans himself. But the design, with its rambling wings, flat roof, cupola, brackets and bays, is so true to the ideal country villa pictured in the books of A. J. Downing and others, that he must certainly have drawn inspiration—at least—from one of those sources. Restoration of the house was begun by the Linn County Historical Society in 1963. It has since become part of the county museum system and is open to the public.

BALDWIN HOUSE 1881: Arcadia, California

E. J. Baldwin—nicknamed "Lucky" for his midas touch—had struck it rich in Northern California, but he settled down northeast of Los Angeles. In 1875 he bought an old Spanish land grant, the *Rancho Santa Anita,* where he planted extensive gardens, began raising horses, and, a few years later, built the fanciful residence shown here.

Originally intended as a guest house, it was supposed to represent the new Queen Anne Style that Baldwin had seen in 1876 at the British Pavilion of the Philadelphia Centennial Exhibition. Though the design by A. A. Bennett, a California architect, has little in common with those English prototypes, it displayed, at a remarkably early date, many of the characteristics that came to define the American Queen Anne house in years to come. These included a break with the box shape, a freer, more "organic" articulation of outer wall shapes, a definite penchant for "picturesque" drama, and a decided taste for outdoor living—as suggested by the wide verandah that completely encircles the house. Most of the ornamental details—gig-cut boards, cross bracing—are, however, more typical of the Gothic and Stick Styles than of the Queen Anne.

What started out as Lucky Baldwin's Victorian gardens eventually became the Los Angeles Arboretum. The house still stands on its original site on the grounds and is accessible to the public, though it is not normally open for inside tours. Its romantically tropical setting and gingerbread trappings, incidentally, made it a television star in the 1970s. It was regularly seen as the exterior of the hotel in *Fantasy Island.*

WARD HOUSE 1882: Seattle, Washington

The Ward House, a rare example of Seattle's Victorian past, has escaped destruction on a number of occasions. Originally sited on the fringe of the central commercial district, it narrowly missed being caught up in the conflagration that razed much of the city in 1889. Later, in 1905, it was consigned to one corner of its large lot to make way for new construction. More recently, in 1986, it was saved from the latest wave of redevelopment when two attorneys, David Leen and Bradford Moore moved it to a safer location and (with some help from an architect, Geoff Lundquist) restored and converted it for use as office space.

The house was originally owned by George Ward, a real estate developer who is thought to have built it himself. Its style is essentially Italianate, as evidenced by its tall proportions, low-pitched hipped roof, and cornice brackets; but some Eastlake touches are also apparent. Though built in what is now downtown Seattle, the plan of the house with its rearward wings and extensions is atypical of town houses as they developed in other cities. Indeed, this survivor seems to be a suburban dwelling that was nearly swallowed up by the enormous expansion that later took place in Seattle. Today it is listed on the National Register and serves as one of the last reminders of its now departed neighbors.

Figure 3: from Bicknell's *Detail, Cottage, and Constructive Architecture*

McPHETERS HOUSE 1882: Santa Cruz, California

This unusual house, probably the only one in Santa Cruz in the French Second Empire Style, was constructed by James Stewart McPheters, a carpenter-builder responsible for a number of other structures still standing in town. Apparently built as his own residence, it derives, at least in part, from a pattern book brought out by A. J. Bicknell & Company in several editions in the 1870s and 80s.

The published plan (fig. 3), credited to C. Graham & Son of Elizabeth, New Jersey, is not in itself unique, and McPheters might well have arrived at a similar design independently; but some of the decorative details in the completed structure—the gable dressings for instance—are too similar to those in the book to be the result of mere coincidence. Whoever the architect was, the design is interesting as an unusual mansardic version of a more or less standard house type: the "gabled-ell" suburban cottage, a form seen also in the Keyes and Torrey Houses in Bellingham and Eureka (pp. 190–191, 193).

R. SHAW HOUSE c.1883: Los Angeles, California

The formal Second Empire Style (as represented by the Stanford-Lathrop and Kamm Houses, pp. 30–31, 38–39) was often transformed by eclecticism and popular taste into something altogether less imposing. The Shaw House shown here is an example of what was called a "French Cottage" in the 1870s and '80s. Its symmetry and some of its detailing derive from the Second Empire, but its smaller scale and homey porch with spindly posts and fancy-worked braces lend it a sense of informality that distinguishes it from its more academic cousins. What is hidden behind the facade and beneath the mansard, moreover, seems to be a rather basic clapboard cottage. The result, despite the French roof and dormers, is a typically American mixture of high style and the vernacular.

Built by a cabinet maker named Richard Shaw in East Los Angeles, the house is quite individual in design. Perhaps because the Mansardic Style was never as popular in the West as in the East, the scattered examples built up and down the Pacific Coast were less prone to homogeneity and casual borrowing than the more common Victorian modes. As a result those that have survived to the present vary widely in appearance. The Bartlett House (pp. 78–79), for example, was built in the same year as the Shaw House and has some similar features—mansard roof, frontal symmetry—but in overall effect the two could hardly be more dissimilar.

The Shaw House is one of a number of formerly endangered Victorians that have found refuge in "Heritage Square" in Highland Park (pp.118–19). Now dedicated as the "Valley Knudsen Garden Residence," it is maintained by the Cultural Heritage Foundation of Southern California and like the other structures in the Square is open for tours.

FRANK BARTLETT HOUSE   1883: Port Townsend, Washington

Port Townsend was founded in 1851 by a small group of settlers who had departed Portland, Oregon, that same year fearing an outbreak of malaria. Because of its strategic location on Puget Sound the new town enjoyed immediate success and soon joined other cities in the scramble to become the northwest terminus of the intercontinental railroad. In the 1880s it experienced a series of booms in anticipation of a rail link to the mainland. But the dream was short lived. The railway never materialized, and by the early 1890s it was evident to even the most optimistic that the bubble had burst. Within a few years Port Townsend had lost most of its population, and further development was effectively curtailed. As a result, much of the architecture built during its peak years is still standing today.

Originally the home of a young entrepreneur named Frank Bartlett, this house dates from a time when the town's hopes were still running high, despite the fact that Tacoma had just become the site of the coveted railhead. Though only 24 years old, Bartlett already had financial interests in a local planing mill and a steel-wire nail plant, and the stylish residence he built on a bluff overlooking the harbor is said to have cost $6,000—a considerable sum for a mere house in those days. Its design has been justifiably admired for its elegant fusion of French and Italian elements—the steep-pitched mansard above and the broad, double-bayed facade below. The names of both the designer and builder, however, are lost to history.

STEVINSON HOUSE 1883: Pacific Grove, California

This is probably one of the last relatively pure examples in the Victorian Gothic mode to be built on the West Coast. Its late date of construction demonstrates how tenacious a hold the style had on the 19th-century imagination. The earliest Gothic houses in America had appeared on the East Coast in the 1830s, and though the style was already declining in fashion by the end of the Civil War, they continued to be built, sporadically, for two more decades in various parts of the country. On the West Coast, houses like this one were still being constructed in Mendocino (and perhaps elsewhere) as late as the 1880s.

This particular incarnation on the Monterey Peninsula, however, suggests that the meaning and function of the style may have begun to change in this latter period. It was built as the summer cottage of a San Joaquin Valley rancher, James J. Stevinson, in the newly developed vacation community of Pacific Grove. The appearance of the style in this setting may indicate that it was employed more for the sake of novelty and nostalgia than as a viable architectural mode in its own right. In the last decades of the 19th century, Gothic houses may already have come to be regarded as quaint period pieces.

FLAVEL HOUSE 1885: Astoria, Oregon

This Victorian landmark at the mouth of the Columbia was built by Captain George Flavel, a self-made millionaire who once served as the first mate of a vessel appropriately named *The Goldhunter.* Flavel had arrived on the West Coast in the late 1840s, and after a brief stay in California travelled north to Oregon where he became one of the first pilots licensed to guide ships across the notorious Columbia River bar. Basing himself in Astoria he gradually acquired a fleet of river and sailing ships that carried freight up and down the river and along the Pacific coast. In time he also acquired extensive interests in real estate, banking, and railroads and became, it is said, the richest man in town.

The mansion he built on the eve of his retirement, is typical of the large villas popular—with those who could afford them—throughout the Victorian period. The term usually refers to the expansive, elegantly appointed, country homes of the rich. But as succinctly defined by A. J. Downing, a "Villa" was simply a country house large enough to require the attention of at least three servants. On this basis the Flavel Mansion with its twenty rooms and seven fireplaces certainly qualifies.

Though the word has Italian connotations, a villa could in fact be couched in any number of styles. The Flavel House, for example, represents the villa in its High Victorian eclectic phase. Along with its Italianate bays and brackets it has a freedom of plan (evidenced by the varied roof forms and wraparound porches) that suggests something of the Queen Anne; but another of the defining feature of that style—a predilection for varied surface textures—is missing here. There is a hint of shingling in the gables, to be sure, but most of the exterior is covered with smooth wood siding carefully matched and painted to mimic masonry construction.

The house's design is credited to Carl W. Leick, a German-born engineer who did a considerable amount of work in the Northwest though he was apparently based in San Francisco. That he was the architect of at least eight lighthouses on the Pacific Coast may partially explain the prominence of the tower that surmounts the Flavel Mansion—a vantage point from which the Captain is said to have spent much time observing his ships after his retirement. His former residence, which is still in very good condition, now serves as the Clatsop County Historical Museum and is open to the public.

VOLLMER HOUSE 1885: San Francisco, California

In California the prodigious talents of the Newsom brothers, Samuel and Joseph, found expression in buildings as far north as Eureka and as far south as Los Angeles. In the early to mid 1880s, however, they were still working primarily in the Bay Area. A number of their designs still stand in Oakland and Marin County, but in San Francisco itself the Vollmer House may be the sole surviving representative of their work. Built a year before the completion of their most famous creation, the William Carson Mansion (pp. 92–95), it too illustrates the Newsom penchant for extravagant ornament and baroque complication of form, but in this case applied to a much smaller canvas, the San Francisco town house.

A comparison of the Vollmer House with earlier examples (pp. 46, 47) shows how much the form had evolved in a few short years. The squared bay on the left, incidentally, was a characteristic feature of San Francisco architecture in the 1880s. Popular because they provided more interior space than the older, slanted bays, these "prows of glass" continued to grow out over the sidewalks until the city passed ordinances limiting their extension.

Earlier in their career the Newsoms had occasionally advertised themselves as "Eastlake Architects," no doubt to suggest to potential clients that they were capable of all the complexity implied by that name. By the time this small extravaganza was finished, however, they seem to have let the label slide. For purposes of trade identification their own name was becoming sufficient unto itself.

WESTERFELD HOUSE 1889: San Francisco, California

Although the town house had become commonplace in San Francisco by the 1880s, the towered villa form was a rarity. The difficulty lay in fitting these broad based, rambling houses into narrow city lots. In the example shown here, built for William Westerfeld, a wealthy baker and confectioner, some of the problems have been solved by modifying the forms themselves. The architect, Henry Geilfuss, simply grafted a tower onto what is essentially an expanded bay-front town house and thus squeezed the villa form into a new vertical shape.

This verticality is enhanced by some embellishments characteristic of San Francisco architecture in this period. The squared bay and linear strips that drop from the cornice line were common in many town houses built in the city in the 1880s. There are also echoes of the Italianate in the decorative brackets, arched windows, classical portico, and asymmetrically placed tower. The final result is a sort of a hybrid: a villa transformed by the constraints of urban space and enlivened by the characteristic mixture of Stick and Italianate ornament that had evolved as part of the "San Francisco Style."

PITKIN HOUSE 1885: Arroyo Grande, California

Charles Pitkin a rancher, builder, and land developer had this towered villa constructed on one of his 500 acres in what later became Arroyo Grande, a small town south of San Luis Obispo. The source of its design is not known, but the tightly integrated plan suggests either that it was the work of an architect or that it was inspired by a pattern book. The house is, in fact, rather similar to one included in Samuel & Joseph Newsom's first portfolio, *Picturesque California Homes* (1884), though many details are different.

In any event, it is an unusually well-preserved example of the villa form in a pre-Queen Anne stage. Its tall proportions (exaggerated a bit in this view) are typical of the 1880s, as is the square tower and applied decorative patterning derived from the Stick Style. The design is especially interesting in comparison to the Westerfeld residence (pp. 87–88), an urban, Italianate approximation of some of the same architectural ideas.

As for construction, the house is built entirely of redwood—inside and out—and its four-story tower is 55 feet high. The structure is said to have cost $9000 to build originally—less than it cost to paint in 1981 according to the current owners. Diana and Ross Cox now operate the former Pitkin residence as The Rose Victorian Inn.

HAAS-LILIENTHAL HOUSE 1886: San Francisco, California

A landmark among landmarks, the Haas-Lilienthal Mansion is one of the largest, most sumptuous Victorians in a city famous for Victorians. It was built for William Haas, a merchant who was originally from Bavaria, and it was later acquired by the wealthy Lilienthal family. More recently it has become the headquarters of the Foundation for San Francisco's Architectural Heritage.

The design, credited to the architect Peter Schmidt, takes advantage of the opportunities for structural elaboration provided by the Queen Anne Style which was still relatively new on the West Coast when this house was built. The irregular roof line, variegated walls, and a new emphasis on the horizontal all lend a dynamic, restless quality to the composition as a whole. There is also evidence of the surface textures that later became a defining characteristic of Queen Anne decoration: some Eastlake and other applied ornament is evident, and the upper story is more or less covered with imbricate shingles. For the most part, however, the wall treatment is still relatively subdued.

The same can be said of the corner tower—another hallmark of the Queen Anne. Its tight integration into one corner of the structure is an acknowledgment of the realities of urban space. For all its size, this is still very much a city house.

WILLIAM CARSON HOUSE 1886: Eureka, California

Fortunes are rapidly accumulated in the United States and the indulgence of one's taste and pride in the erection of a countryseat of great size and cost is becoming a favorite mode of expending wealth.
————A. J. Downing: *The Architecture of Country Houses*

By the mid 1880s Eureka had begun to supplant its rival, Arcata, as the dominant city on Humboldt Bay and was undergoing a boom that continued in fits and starts throughout the 1890s. Of the many elaborate residences that appeared in the town during this period, none is more famous than the Carson Mansion. Built by one of the area's most prosperous lumbermen, and designed by two of San Francisco's more uninhibited architects, it stands, a century after its construction, as one of the landmarks of American Victorian architecture.

William McKendrie Carson, who built this monument, was born in 1825 in Charlotte County, New Brunswick where he worked as a logger until he was drawn to California by the gold rush. He arrived in San Francisco early in 1850 and spent two unsuccessful seasons in the gold fields before establishing full-time logging operations in the Humboldt Bay area. From rough-and-ready beginnings he went on to build sawmills, buy ships, and send boatloads of California redwood down the coast. By the 1880s he was a millionaire and was ready to build a proper millionaire's home.

Samuel and Joseph Newsom, the architects he commissioned to design the house, were also originally from Canada, though they were raised in San Francisco. They had begun their careers, as draftsmen in the architectural office of an older brother, and in 1878 they formed a partnership of their own that became one of the most productive sources of building design in 19th-century California. By 1884, when some of their work was beginning to sprout up in Eureka, they were already well established in the San Francisco Bay Area and had developed a certain reputation for their extravagant, sometimes slightly mad conceptions—a description that fits the design they conjured up for William Carson.

Employing the towered villa as a point of departure, they created a sort of grand synthesis in which a little of all the previous Victorian Styles were combined in a single structure. There is more than a hint of the Gothic in the steep pitch of the gables; something of the Italianate in the tower and extended bracketing; a mansard roof is all but hidden behind ubiquitous Stick and Eastlake detailing; and everything is built on a Queen Anne frame—rambling, irregular,

93

and decidedly "picturesque." The scale of the house too, is impressive. With its five-story tower, sweeping verandah, numerous wings, bays, and balconies it gave the Newsoms unprecedented scope to express their proclivities for baroque ornament and bold overstatement of form.

Why Carson built so extravagantly has been the subject of various theories. One claim—that he wanted to keep his employees working during a depression in the forest industry—may not be as farfetched as it sounds: the house was two years in the building, and the labor alone is said to have cost upwards of $75,000. This explanation accords, moreover, with the tradition that Carson was an extremely popular figure in Eureka, liked and admired by everyone in town—a reputation hardly likely to have befallen a man who genuinely acted the part of a "lumber baron," as he is almost invariably described.

Another suggestion is that the lavishness of the mansion was intended to advertise the possibilities of wood as a construction material—and, intentionally or not, it does just that. Built entirely of local redwood (except for some interior work that employed more exotic timbers) it is a practical demonstration that the wooden house was capable of a degree of grandeur and complexity more commonly associated with masonry construction.

However, a more straightforward rationale for the complexity of the design and construction is also possible. It may be that Carson and the Newsoms simply wanted to create something spectacular and between them were enviably endowed with the talent and money necessary to carry it off. It may also be that each of these explanations contains some validity. They do not, at least, contradict one another, and the mansion does seem particularly capable of eliciting and absorbing varying interpretations.

Contemporary opinion, for example, tends to regard it either as an instance of high camp, or as an egregious expression of personal egotism and conspicuous consumption—not to mention callous disregard for nature and her materials. In acquiring the fortune that allowed him to build so immoderately (we are reminded) Carson deforested entire tracts of Northern California timberland.

Modern scruples aside, however, the house can be seen as emblematic of Victorian architecture and society as a whole. At once vulgar in its ostentation and admirable in its accomplishment, it has been characterized in adjectives that range from "monstrous" to "magnificent." No matter what the judgment on it, however, it has generally commanded at least grudging respect for the scale of its ambition and the sheer energy and inventiveness of its performance.

Today the Carson Mansion is a private club, exquisitely maintained, but not generally open to the public.

GEORGE L. KIMBALL HOUSE 1887: National City, California

That houses like this one continued to appear until well into the 1890s is proof of the enduring hold the Italianate Style had on Victorian taste. Already a little out of fashion when it was built, the Kimball House is nonetheless a fine performance on a favorite theme—the transitional box enlivened by Italianate styling.

Designed by an architect named Curtis, it was built by George Kimball, one of five brothers who had purchased a former Spanish land grant, the *Rancho de la Nacion,* in 1868. This ambitious clan pooled their energies in an effort to make National City, as they named it, the leading community on San Diego Bay. Between them they owned a brick foundry, planing mill, even their own narrow-gauge railway. One of the brothers, Frank, moreover, played an important role in helping Southern California establish its citrus, grape, and olive growing industries.

This house (George Kimball's third on the ranch) was built when the brothers' power and influence in the area was at its peak. In an effort to bring the transcontinental railroad to town, however, they over-extended themselves by deeding away much of their property and financing many of the public buildings in the community. When the long-awaited terminus was awarded to San Bernardino instead of National City, the boom was over, and the brothers' fortunes began to wane. Laura Kimball, the last member of the family to occupy this house, lived to see it sold for back taxes in 1941.

PHILLIPS HOUSE 1887: Los Angeles, California

During the Spanish and Mexican periods and in the first two decades after American annexation, Los Angeles remained little more than a sleepy cow town: by the end of the 1860s it still numbered only about 5000 people. From the 1870s on, however, it grew steadily, and toward the end of the following decade its population expanded exponentially due to a land rush engineered by railroad interests. At the peak of a rate war manufactured to draw new people to the area, a one-way ticket from Kansas City cost just one dollar. In 1887, when the house shown here was built, the former village had become a city of nearly 100,000 people.

During the building booms of the era several new residential neighborhoods were plotted out around the outskirts of the original settlement. Most of these have undergone radical modernization since then, and others have disappeared altogether; but Angelino Heights—once only a short streetcar ride from downtown Los Angeles—has managed to retain at least a hint of its original character. Until fairly recently benign neglect was the chief factor in the survival of many of its older houses, but in the past decade or so energetic restoration efforts by individual owners have brought a late 19th-century bloom back to the neighborhood. One street in particular, Carroll Avenue, has become the center of this activity: in a single block it displays a dozen or so well-preserved Victorians in various stages of restoration.

At least one of these, the Phillips House, is typical of an early phase of the Queen Anne popular in California in the late 1880s. Its open, unboxed gables and wings with cutaway corners are characteristic of houses in transition from the earlier Stick Style. In addition it is decorated with ornament of a distinct type. The gridded diaperwork that embellishes the gables, the sunburst motifs, the rows of flat disks, the linear patterns incised in the window surrounds—all are typical of the applied surface decoration known as "Eastlake."

More a decorative mode than a style per se, it derived both from the simpler patterning of the Stick Style and from the furniture motifs of an English designer, Charles Locke Eastlake. The Englishman was quick to repudiate the American fashion that had appropriated his name: "extravagant and bizarre" was his assessment of it. But the term stuck, and in California at least, the distinctive ornament became a mainstay of Queen Anne decorative schemes. By comparison with more abundantly decorated examples like the Hale House (pp. 118–119), this one is adorned quite modestly.

J. MILTON CARSON HOUSE 1887: Eureka, California

This impressive house would have been even more so on almost any other block in the country. But fate has placed it directly across the street from another Carson House (pp. 92–95)—the premier example of Victorian architecture on the West Coast—and the Younger Carson, as it is sometimes called, inevitably suffers by comparison.

Still, if one keeps one's back to the larger house, this one has a lot to recommend it. Designed by Samuel and Joseph Newsom for one of the sons of lumber baron William Carson, it is a splendid example of the towered Queen Anne and displays the full range of structural and ornamental features associated with that style: onion-domed tower, multiple gables, shingled panels and Eastlake decorative touches to name just a few.

But another look at the larger house across the street is enough to set the comparisons spinning again and to cause speculation about what it must have been like for a man to live perpetually—and at certain times of the year literally—in his father's shadow.

EASTLAKE COTTAGE 1887: Santa Cruz, California

Once owned by a local lumberman named Mark Whittle, this cottage represents a distinct house-type that was evidently rather popular in Northern California in the 1880s. As in the example illustrated here, houses of this sort were typically built on a story-and-a-half, raised-basement plan, and their distinguishing features included a hipped roof with central gable, a symmetrical facade with centered entryway (often recessed between flanking bays), and a predilection for turned and cut Eastlake ornament.

This house, constructed by a builder, J. Hart of San Jose, may be something of a rarity in Santa Cruz: either very few like it were built there, or very few have survived. Similar ones can be found in greater numbers in towns like Napa and, especially, Eureka. Other examples of the type can be seen in the W. S. Clark residence (pp. 104–105) and in a design included in Joseph & Samuel Newsom's first pattern book (fig. 4). The origins of the form are unclear, but its symmetrical arrangement and tendency to employ extensive ornamental bracketing suggest a relation to the double-bayed Italianate house.

Figure 4: Plate 24, *Picturesque California Homes*

W. S. CLARK HOUSE 1888: Eureka, California

This elaborately detailed house was originally the residence of William Squire Clark, a real estate developer who was twice elected mayor of Eureka. It was constructed by F. B. Butterfield, a local contractor who may also have designed it since no evidence of another architect has yet turned up. Like the Eastlake cottage (shown on pp. 102–103), this house is representative of a distinct house-type popular in Northern California in the 1880s—particularly in Eureka to judge from the number that have survived there.

This example is especially notable for the ornate bargeboards that decorate its gables (three of them in all) and for the wealth of turned woodwork that enriches the portico set between the squared bays. Most of this ornament can be loosely categorized as "Eastlake," but the bracketing beneath the eaves harks back to the Italianate, as does the round-headed window set into the gable end. The house has been in use as a private residence throughout its life, and has been exceptionally well maintained. Both interior and exterior appear to be essentially as they were when the structure was completed a hundred years ago.

ALONZO BROWN HOUSE 1888: Oakland, Oregon

Oakland, the first permanent white settlement in the Umpqua Valley, was founded in 1846 by two families who were halted by winter while attempting to reach the Willamette country further north. At first the community was scarcely more than a rural settlement and stage stop, but after the Oregon & California railroad arrived in 1872, the town enjoyed a modest boom that lasted until the turn of the century. Today it retains a distinct 19th-century flavor, and has recently been declared a National Historic District.

The house shown here—one of several Victorians in the community—was built for Alonzo F. Brown, a Douglas County farmer who donated land for the railroad right-of-way in the Oakland vicinity. This may have been something of a coup, since the new town that resulted was built, in effect, on his land. The depot became the center of activity in the community and most of the wooden buildings in town were moved a mile or so from their original sites to be near it. Brown was appointed station agent by the railroad, and like C. D. Drain Sr. (pp. 164–165), who struck a similar deal with the Oregon & California, seems to have made a comfortable living from the general store he opened. He died, incidentally, in 1937 at the age of 101.

The various farmhouses he occupied during his long life all seem to have been couched in basic vernacular, but his town house was constructed in the Italianate Style that was still fashionable in rural communities at this relatively late date. On the evidence of a period photograph the main structure appears to be essentially the same today as when it was first built, but the extended porch with its classical columns and pediment is reported to have been added in the 1930s.

J. M. BUNN HOUSE c.1888: Yamhill, Oregon

Originally built by a farmer, William Ball, in 1860, this house was later acquired by John Marion Bunn who enlarged it in 1888. Bunn was also a farmer, the son of a homesteader who had come from Tennessee in 1851, but he also served on the city council and as mayor of Yamhill, a small town in the hill country west of the Willamette Valley. The distinctive mansard roof was probably added to the house immediately after he purchased it, though it has been suggested that it was already in place by the late 1870s. Whatever the actual date, the fashionable, highly visible addition was a relatively simple but very effective way of adding distinction to what was probably at first just another vernacular farmhouse. The question is: why go to the trouble, especially in such a small town?

A hint may be found a few blocks away in the Lee Laughlin House (pp. 56–57), which contains one of the most elegant blendings of Gothic Revival and Italianate elements in the Northwest. And the conclusion (bolstered by similar evidence in other small towns) may be, simply, that high style begets high style.

LACY HOUSE 1888: Pacific Grove, California

A facade as romantic as this one might be expected to have a story behind it, and—true or not—the one that has grown up around this house has all the right ingredients for melodrama: a proper Englishman, a ruined Southern Belle, a love child, and, of course, the romantically isolated cottage itself.

As the tale goes, William Lacy, an English engineer and dabbler in architecture had a wife and five children in Los Angeles, but secretly had another home in secluded Pacific Grove for his mistress and their daughter. His inamorata, Emma Murdoch, was the daughter of a Virginia plantation owner who had lost everything in the Civil War. Adrift in Los Angeles in the late 1870s, she became close friends with Lacy, and some years later took up residence with their infant daughter in the house he built on the Monterey Peninsula. Lacy (who was also a yachtsman) died a few years later of pneumonia precipitated by a boating accident, and "the Widow Murdoch," as she was known in the strait-laced vacation community, lived on in the house until her daughter was raised.

Questions of veracity aside, the story certainly accords with the romantic character of this oversized cottage: with its multiple gables it might have been drawn straight from the pages of a Gothic Novel. And it does look like the work of an Englishman: there is more than a suggestion of Elizabethan half-timbering in the heavy stick work that decorates the gables and top-heavy tower; and other touches—the pointed Gothic arch of the entryway for example—distinguish it from the run of American houses built up and down the coast in the same period. Restored in 1983, it is now the Green Gables Inn, a bed and breakfast establishment.

BLAIR HOUSE 1888: Mendocino, California

Mendocino began as a lumber town in the 1850s, but the stands of virgin timber that brought it initial prosperity were almost entirely depleted within a few decades. For most of the 20th century it survived as little more than a picturesque and isolated spot on California's northern coast, but in the 1960s it was rediscovered by refugees from the fast lane and has since become a pleasant and cultivated backwater, home to improbable numbers of musicians and artists.

Thanks to the extensive use of redwood in its early buildings and the historical status granted the entire community a few years back, a good sampling of Mendocino's 19th-century architecture remains intact. The influence of the many New Englanders who settled in the area is particularly evident in some interesting local adaptations of the salt box and the Cape Cod cottage, but the dominant stylistic note is struck by the Gothic Revival.

This architectural mode was employed almost from the day the town was founded, and relatively pure examples were still being built there as late as the early 1880s. The house pictured here dates from a few years later and has taken on some new flourishes, but its steep gables and board-and-batten siding still proclaim its origins. The brackets, bays, and window hoods, however, bespeak the influence of the Italianate, and the shingle cladding and irregular plan indicate the stirrings of a relatively new style—the Queen Anne. If, as some authorities suggest, the latter was simply a high-Victorian elaboration of the Gothic Revival by way of intermediate styles, this eclectic example may be as good an illustration of the transition as any to be found on the West Coast.

The house was built for Elisha Blair—former state of Mainer, retired mill worker, and dabbler in finance—by John D. Johnson, a carpenter-builder credited with the construction of several other interesting residences around town. Originally from England, Johnson had arrived in Mendocino in the early 1870s shortly after a major fire swept the community and created a definite need for builders. After the reconstruction he took over the local undertaker's establishment where, no doubt, his carpentry skills were also put to good use.

BENJAMIN YOUNG HOUSE 1888: Astoria, Oregon

In the last quarter of the 19th century the population of Astoria swelled as a wave of Scandinavian immigrants began arriving in the area. Benjamin Young, who built the house shown here, was a particularly successful representative of this group. Born in Sweden, he arrived in Astoria with his wife in 1874 just as the town was developing as the most important salmon-canning center on the Columbia. Young was quick to realize the potential of the industry and in relatively short order set up his own packing plant. In time he developed a thriving export business and had interests in canning operations as far away as Alaska and British Columbia.

Some measure of his success may be guaged by the expansive, fashionable residence he built for his family. The house is an early example in the Queen Anne Style and displays a persistent characteristic of late Victorian design—a tendency to avoid continuous flat surfaces. In this example variation has been achieved by employing vertical and horizontal strips to divide the walls into sections—a device carried over from the Stick Style. As the Queen Anne house developed over time, similar effects were obtained by breaking up wall surfaces with decorative panels or bands of patterned shingles, and—in still more extreme forms—by making the exterior surfaces themselves ever more complex. With its modest Eastlake sunbursts and shingled turret, the Young House is still quite strait-laced by comparison. Who designed the house is not known, and the contractor who built it is remembered only by his last name—Palmer.

WILLIAM HENSHAW HOUSE c.late 1880s: Oakland, California

Not much is known about the early history of this house except that it was once the residence of William Henshaw, one of the sons-in-law of Hiram Tubbs, a wealthy and prominent hotel owner in Oakland. Nonetheless, it is interesting as a well-preserved representative of the Queen Anne Style that began to dominate the suburban areas of the East Bay in the late 1880s and early 90s.

By this time (in the San Francisco area at least) the characteristic features of the style were becoming more or less standardized. Two general tendencies that are particularly apparent in the Henshaw House are the variegated roof and wall forms, and a new emphasis on shingles and applied ornament to break up continuous exterior surfaces. The tower, or something suggesting it, was also becoming *de regeur* and was added to even the most modest suburban dwellings whenever possible. In this not-so-modest example the tower has become a turret that projects like a medieval bartizan from the angled first-story bay on which it rests. A very similar arrangement can be seen in the Hale House in Los Angeles (pp. 118–119) which resembles the Henshaw residence in some other respects as well.

HALE HOUSE 1888: Los Angeles, California

This immaculately restored residence is one of several 19th-century structures that have found refuge from vandals, termites, and condominium developers in Heritage Square, an outdoor museum maintained by the Cultural Heritage Foundation of Southern California. Collecting old houses in a sort of park may seem like an extreme response to the problem of historical preservation, and some purists within the movement have been troubled by its implications. But in Los Angeles, which has experienced nearly constant change since the 1880s, such a strategy may be the only way of guaranteeing the continued survival of some remnants of its architectural past. Of the several buildings in the Square, the Hale House is particularly emblematic of these concerns since it was itself a product of early land development in the city and in its hundred-year life has twice been moved to make room for the broad bottom of progress.

Though it takes its name from its longest residents, James and Bessie Hale, the house was originally owned by a real estate developer named George Washburn Morgan. It was thought for a while to have been designed by Joseph Newsom, but this attribution has not been substantiated. It may be reasonable to assume, however, that Morgan played some role in its construction. He was the original subdivider of Highland Park, one of Los Angeles' first suburbs, and this, his own residence, has all the earmarks of a developer's flagship, complete to the initials "G. M." incised in a plaque beneath the central gable.

In design the house is a robust example in the Queen Anne Revival Style, which had become quite popular by the late 1880s, particularly in larger cities. In contrast to some earlier West Coast houses that explored the new style rather more tentatively, this example displays a full commitment to all the characteristics commonly associated with the Queen Anne: complex roof and wall shapes, an eclectic appropriation of ornamental features from earlier styles, a taste for drama and asymmetry, and (as evidenced by the variety of materials that cover its exterior) a positive aversion for smooth, unrelieved surfaces. In addition, some of the individual elements within the composition have taken on a restless life of their own—another hallmark of the Queen Anne. The front chimney, for instance, grows right through a gable and reemerges out of the roof, and a top-heavy, second-story turret straddles the angled bay at one side of the house.

The Hale House is also a rarity in that it has been repainted in its original Victorian colors—determined by a careful analysis of chips taken from different parts of the structure. Like the other buildings in Heritage Square (pp. 76 – 77), it is open for public tours.

BAIR-STOKES HOUSE 1888: Arcata, California

Humboldt Bay was first developed in the early 1850s as a coastal supply point for the Trinity River gold fields. However, it soon became important in its own right as a lumber center—an identity it still retains, though the redwoods have been mostly logged away. The two towns on the bay, Arcata and Eureka, vied for dominance in the area until the latter began to win out by virtue of its superior harbor. During the period of contention, however, a number of fine homes were built in Arcata, and because the area was not significantly developed in later years, many of these have survived to the present.

One of the most extravagant is the house shown here. It was built for a local doctor, Fred H. Bangs, but is better known by the names of two families who have occupied it, successively, for nearly a century. In the early period Thomas Bair, who acquired the house in 1898, was perhaps its most colorful occupant. Described as a "self-made man," he was orphaned at the age of nine but later became a millionaire as a result of holdings he acquired in the local timber industry.

The design has been attributed to Samuel & Joseph Newsom, the architects of the William Carson Mansion (pp. 92–95) which stands across the bay in Eureka, but this has not been substantiated. The actual construction may have been the work of Shephard Hall, a local contractor known to have built several other residences in the area. Whoever was responsible for the design created a virtual paradigm of the Queen Anne: it contains most of the features commonly associated with the style and then some. The richly spindled porch with its horseshoe-arched entry is a particularly noteworthy detail, and the flared, shingled walls mark a significant point of departure from the sharp-edged, linear geometries that characterized earlier Victorian design.

JACKSON-MATTHEWS HOUSE 1888: Arcata, California

By the late 1880s the corner-towered Queen Anne was well on its way to attaining the popularity that made it a standard house type in the following decade. Inspired by monumental examples like the Haas-Lilienthal and Carson Mansions (pp. 90–91, 92–95) scaled-down versions of the "picturesque towered villa" began to appear in more modest dimensions and at more egalitarian prices. In the 1890s it was not unusual to find even single story residences that boasted some facsimile of a tower; but two-story versions were more common. Typically these were hipped-roof cottages with a tower on one side of the facade, and, to balance the composition, a prominent front gable on the other. In practice, variations on this basic theme were endless and the degree of elaboration depended only on the taste and budget of the owner.

And the skill of the builder. In the late Victorian era (as in other phases of architectural history in America) the vast majority of dwellings owed their design as well as their construction to the ubiquitous builder-contractor. The Jackson House, for instance, appears to have been constructed by Theodore Dean, who may also have designed it. It is one of two residences—identical except that their plans are reversed—placed at opposite ends of the same block like towered bookends. In form this example is typical of many built in the late 1880s, but with some interesting differences in details. The boxed-off front gable, the Palladian window in the attic, and the extensive shingling (which effectively excludes other wall ornament) are more characteristic of the Queen Anne in a later stage of development. The flared walls and overhanging second-story wings are also quite sophisticated.

The house was originally the home of yet another transplanted state of Mainer, Elisha B. Jackson, who came to California looking for gold but ended up mining redwood. He had already passed his share of a successful logging and milling operation on to his son by the time this residence was built. In the nearly 100 years that have passed since then, the house has been owned by only one other family, the Matthews.

SESSIONS HOUSE 1888: Los Angeles, California

After establishing a solid reputation in San Francisco and Eureka, the architects Samuel & Joseph Newsom next turned their attention to Southern California. In 1886 they opened a branch office in Los Angeles, which was then undergoing its first real building boom, and Joseph, the younger of the two brothers, headed this operation up for the next several years. Of the residences he designed in this period, the Sessions House is perhaps the most interesting that has survived.

Like the Phillips House (pp. 98–99) it was built in Angelino Heights, a residential neighborhood not far from downtown Los Angeles. Its design, which later appeared in a Newsom pattern book, is still very much in the Queen Anne tradition, but some of its features point—already—in a new direction. The extensive shingle cladding and the incorporation of the corner turret into the main body of the structure suggest that Newsom was very much aware of the new Shingle Style that was beginning to attain popularity in the East. On a more abstract level the design of the facade is also interesting for its almost compulsive repetition of the triangle and the circle. The spare sophistication of this house contains little to connect its architect with the baroque complexities of the Carson Mansion (pp. 92–95) completed just two years before.

SHERMAN-GILBERT HOUSE c.1889: San Diego, California

John Sherman, a real estate developer, built this house during San Diego's boom period in the late 1880s. The other half of the name derives from Bess and Gertrude Gilbert, art patrons who are remembered for the elaborate receptions they staged for visiting celebrities. The design is credited to Comstock and Trotsche, an architectural team responsible for several other finely-wrought Victorians in the San Diego area.

This example of their work employs a decorative technique that developed out of the Stick Style—so named for the characteristic stick patterning used to embellish many Victorian houses. "Stick-work" of the simplest type took the form of vertical and diagonal "bracing" applied decoratively over horizontal siding, and was often lauded for its honesty in portraying on the outer skin of the structure the frame skeleton that lay beneath it. However, as time passed this emphasis on "truthfulness" gave way to a desire for applied surface decoration for its own sake—as in this unusual example. Though some remnants of basic stick patterning are still apparent, most of the surface of the house is covered with decorative panels, scroll cut in a variety of motifs.

The Sherman-Gilbert House is another Victorian that owes its continued existence to a local preservation group. Scheduled for demolition in the late 1960s, it was purchased, relocated in San Diego's Old Town district, and restored by a group known as S.O.H.O. Since then it has become the nucleus of Heritage Park, where several other historic buildings have found relative safety from the forces that threaten old houses elsewhere.

L. M. SMITH HOUSE 1894: Ferndale, California

This unusually decorated house was originally owned by Lucius Miles Smith, a barrel maker employed by one of Ferndale's several creameries. It displays the sort of ornament, usually called Eastlake, that was applied liberally to many of the residential and commercial structures built in the town during its heyday in the 1880s and 90s. This example is replete with graphic sunbursts, bull's eyes, stars, rosettes, strips, bars, and who-knows-whats applied in the gables, on the window surrounds, porch frieze, and bay windows—everywhere, it seems, except on the walls themselves. The porch also has turned posts, balusters and a spindle course, the bay windows are bracketed, and the edges of the house have been decorated with quoins. The structure onto which all this has been applied is essentially the same cross-gabled plan seen in the Peters-Wintermeier and Crellin Houses (pp. 34–35, 36–37). In this case, though, the basic plan has been altered by the addition of a large two-story bay—almost a wing in itself—on one side of the house.

RALSTON HOUSE 1889: Albany, Oregon

This house, one of the best preserved representatives of the Eastlake Style in the Northwest, was originally built for John Ralston, a veteran of the Oregon Trail who later became an insurance man. He had come to Oregon from Indiana with his parents in 1847 when he was still a boy; and though the family travelled the overland trail in typical pioneer fashion, John and his two brothers eventually went into business rather than farming. In time, Ralston became an insurance broker and settled in Albany, a small town on the Willamette River 25 miles upstream from Salem.

The town had been founded in 1848 when the Monteith brothers, Walter and Thomas, arrived from upstate New York and purchased the site for $400 and a Cayuse pony, and it grew steadily as it became by turns a riverboat landing, stage stop, and railroad center. By the late 1880s, when the Ralston House was built, it was an important agricultural, manufacturing, and shipping hub in the Willamette Valley.

Though neither the architect—if any—nor the builder have been identified, this story-and-a-half, raised-basement house is notable for the wealth of applied ornament that covers much of its exterior. Particularly fine Stick and Eastlake detailing appears in the porch and gable work of the facade, and recurring motifs decorate most of the house. There are, for example, at least three variations on the sunburst. The thin battens applied at the tops of the window hoods suggest, once again, the relationship between Stick-Style patterning and the older board and batten tradition of the Gothic Revival. The Fort Dalles Surgeon's Quarters (pp. 22–23) is decorated in much the same way. In addition the angled, corner bay lends a "picturesque" note to the facade, and the second story pavilion (a small tower in effect) harmonizes nicely with the modest scale of the rest of the house.

Figure 5: Design No. 41, *The Cottage Souvenir No. 2*

HOCHSTEDLER HOUSE c.1889: Albany, Oregon

This handsome residence in the Stick-Eastlake-Queen Anne tradition is interesting as an example of pattern-book architecture. It was based on a design by George Franklin Barber, an architect who began his career in DeKalb, Illinois and later established an extensive mail-order practice in Knoxville, Tennessee. The design was initially realized in the construction of the C. E. Bradt House (built in Dekalb in 1887 or '88) and was subsequently published both in an 1888 edition of the trade journal *Carpentry and Building* and in a sampler of designs that the architect brought out himself that same year. When his second portfolio, *The Cottage Souvenir No. 2.,* appeared a little less than three years later, Barber claimed that this design, "No. 41" (fig. 5), had already given rise to more than one hundred other houses in the United States and Canada.

One of those, presumably, was this example in Albany which is a mirror reversal of the original design. George Hochstedler (a building contractor as it happens) evidently saw the plan in one of its published forms, ordered working drawings from Barber's offices in the East, and build this, his own residence, with the construction resources at his disposal. Records in Albany show that it cost $6,000—considerably more than other houses built in town in the same period—so it may be, as seems often to have been the case with builders, that Hochstedler meant it to advertise the capabilities of his firm.

In any case, all this suggests some of the workings of mail-order architecture in the latter decades of the 19th century. By publishing a portfolio or "pattern book," an architect could simultaneously advertise the quality of his work, generate new commissions from afar, and realize repeated profits by selling working plans *ad infinitum.* And equipped with such a book of designs, a good builder could function as a surrogate architect in a small town. Though the practice of making plans and specifications available through the mail dates at least to the publication of Cleaveland and Backus Brother's *Village and Farm Cottages* (1856), the mail-order concept was carried to its logical extreme by architects like Barber who conducted a large share of their business on the basis of written correspondence.

133

STARRETT HOUSE 1889: Port Townsend, Washington

In its bid for ascendancy among cities on Puget Sound, Port Townsend underwent a final spurt of growth in the late 1880s. Its population soared to a new high, and a series of building booms ensued. Of the houses built during this period, many were the work of George Starrett, a carpenter from Maine who became by turns a builder, contractor, brick manufacturer and sawmill operator. By his own account, he constructed no less than 350 houses in Port Townsend within four years of his arrival in 1885.

Though the house shown here was nominally built as a gift for Mrs. Starrett, it was also intended, no doubt, as a showcase for her husband's talents. Inside, it was a mixture of the lavish and the progressive. There were, for example, no fireplaces—a testament to the builder's faith in the central-heating system he had installed. But there were also touches of opulence: a free-hanging stairway that spiraled dramatically up the tower, and Otto Chapman's allegorical ceiling paintings of the Four Seasons—said to have shocked polite society by their personification of "Winter" as a female nude.

On the outside, the sharp-edged vertical and diagonal geometries of the Stick Style are in evidence in the two main wings of the house; but its overall character is established by the dramatic, octagonal tower—a touch of the Queen Anne. In fact if it were not for this impressive, four-story structure, the house might have been fairly ordinary in appearance. It was originally painted, incidentally, in contrasting shades of green—evidently a very trendy color scheme in the late 1880s.

135

LONG-WATERMAN HOUSE 1889: San Diego, California

An unusually sophisticated example in the Queen Anne Style, this house was built during San Diego's late 1880s building boom. It was briefly the residence of John S. Long, one of the founders of the Coronado Fruit Package Company, but was acquired in 1890 by Mrs. Robert Whitney Waterman whose husband became governor of California that same year.

The design, by D. B. Benson of the firm of Benson & Reif, takes full advantage of the building techniques of the late Victorian period to achieve a free-flowing composition of undulating wall shapes and irregular roof forms. Within this framework, eclectic stylistic touches have been applied. The vergeboard that dresses the front gable, for example, looks back to the Gothic Revival, while the eyebrow dormer anticipates the Shingle Style. However, Queen Anne elements like the patterned shingling, rounded bays, and wraparound porch sound the dominant notes.

MARBLE HOUSE c.1889: Seattle, Washington

Victorian houses have become a rarity in Seattle. The reasons are various, but most have to do with the rapid pace of urban development that took place in this, the largest city in the Northwest. At first the town showed little promise of the regional dominance it later achieved. Though founded in 1852, its population remained less than 1,000 for the next 20 years. Port Townsend rivaled it as a shipping point, and Tacoma bested it in the competition to become the site of the coveted Northern Pacific Railroad terminus. In 1889, moreover, a devastating fire destroyed much of Seattle's downtown area. This disaster actually spurred new growth—the city's population soared to 35,000 in 1890—but reconstruction efforts had the effect of displacing housing to the nearer suburbs to make way for civic and commercial buildings. These new neighborhoods, in turn, were redeveloped when even more rapid expansion overtook the city in the twentieth century.

The house shown here is one of the last Victorian survivors in the Queen Anne Hill section of the city. This area is particularly favored for residences because of its admirable views of Puget Sound and the central district. Its name, in fact, derives from the many Queen Anne houses that dotted its terraces in the late 19th and early 20th centuries. Of the history of this reminder from the period, little is known except that one of its first owners was a woman named Rachel Marble. It is thought to have been built in 1889, though its squared porch posts (assuming they are not remodeled additions) suggest a later date of construction.

WALKER-AMES HOUSE 1889: Port Gamble, Washington

Built originally for the resident manager of the Pope & Talbot Sawmill at Port Gamble, this somber-looking Queen Anne still serves as a residence today. The company, the mill, and the town itself were founded by three lumbermen from Maine—A. J. Pope, William Talbot, and Cyrus Walker. They arrived on the West Coast in 1852 and a year later established a settlement on Puget Sound. Their new enterprise, which was originally based on supplying lumber for San Francisco's unprecedented building boom, was a success from the start, and in time the company became one of the giants in the forest industry with milling operations and real estate interests in various parts of the West.

Port Gamble, which is still owned by the company, was pattterned after its founders' home town, East Machias, Maine. In addition to the residence shown here, a number of other early structures have been restored in recent years. These include some interesting vernacular Gothic and Italianate houses and a perfect copy of a New England church.

JACOB JENNE HOUSE 1889: Coupeville, Washington

Coupeville, the first permanent white settlement on Puget Sound's Whidbey Island, dates from 1852 when it was established by Captain Thomas Coupe. Though never very large, the town prospered well enough from farming and fishing during the 19th century to leave a capsule history of Victorian House Styles behind. Surviving examples range from the Gothic Revival through the Italianate, and there is even an example or two in the French Mansard and Queen Anne Styles—a remarkable assortment for such a small place.

The residence shown here is in the Italian mode and was built by Jacob Jenne, one member of a sizeable family in the area. It is illustrative of a tendency in relatively isolated communities to graft high-style elements onto vernacular forms. No doubt the close proximity of Port Townsend had some influence on architecture in Coupeville. The cornice brackets in this house, for instance, seem to be stock items that also appear in several houses in the larger town across the Admiralty Inlet.

Much of the central Whidbey area is now a part of a unique historical reserve administered by the National Park Service, though most of the houses are still privately owned. The Jenne residence is now a bed and breakfast inn.

EZRA MEEKER HOUSE 1890: Puyallup, Washington

This high-style Italianate mansion, designed by the Tacoma firm of Farrell & Darmer, was built by one of the most successful pioneers ever to take the Oregon Trail west. Ezra Meeker, who was born in Ohio in 1830, gathered up his wife and young son in 1852 and took the Old National Road to Kansas City where it met the overland trail to the Pacific Northwest. After a stay in Kalama, Washington, where he worked timber (and was once swept down the Columbia all the way to Astoria on a log raft), he settled in Puyallup, near Tacoma, where he devoted his energies to the unlikely enterprise of hop farming. Thanks to his inventive talents and the fertility of the soil, however, the area became known as the "Hop Capital of the World." At the height of his success Meeker, the "Hop King," had an income of a half million dollars a year.

However, insect infestation and a financial panic in the 1890s brought ruin to the empire he had established, and he devoted the rest of his life to marking and publicizing the Oregon Trail. These efforts, which included retracing by car, train, and plane the route he had originally taken with ox and wagon, were rewarded three years after his death when the trail was declared a National Historical Highway in 1931.

The Meeker Mansion is notable for its widow's walk, porte cochere (or carriage porch) and Eastlake interior. Still in good repair, it is maintained by the Ezra Meeker Historical Society and is open to the public.

WILL JENNE HOUSE 1890: Coupeville, Washington

Once the residence of Will Jenne (a member of a family that seems to have been quite numerous in Coupeville in the 19th century) this house is perhaps the best representative in the central Whidbey Island area of the building modes of the later Victorian period. Stick and Queen Anne influences are evident both in the decorative details and in the irregular massing and meandering walls of the structure itself. Its basic plan, an arrangement of two flanking wings around a towerlike central block, is somewhat reminiscent of the Starrett House in Port Townsend (pp. 134–135). Behind these high-style borrowings, however, the lingering presence of a simpler, more basic house can still be seen. Like many other residences in the district, this one demonstrates how easily vernacular structures could be fitted out with fashionable new trapppings. The Jacob Jenne House (pp. 142–143), built only a year before this one, was couched in the Italianate Style, but it might well have been the work of the same builder.

HOLMES HOUSE c.1890: Astoria, Oregon

Like his close contemporary Benjamin Young (pp. 114–115), Gustavus Holmes was a Swedish immigrant who attained success in the salmon-packing industry, an important part of Astoria's economy in the closing decades of the 19th century. He had arrived in the community in 1875 after farming in Kansas for several years and initially worked as a salmon fisherman. However, he soon became involved in one of the area's first fishermen's cooperatives, and in 1882 he formed a partnership with Benjamin Young to build a packing plant in British Columbia. They later sold the operation for a healthy profit, and, returning to Astoria, Holmes helped found the Scandinavian-American Bank and built the residence shown here on a hill that now bears his name.

No information has survived on who designed the house, but it seems likely that it was the work of a carpenter-builder rather than a schooled architect. Its design is rather individual, though it displays some definite Italianate and Stick leanings. Its central bay and gable, corner tower, and pedimented porch entry, moreover, are somewhat reminiscent of similar features seen in the Flavel House (pp. 82–83)—the most elaborate residence in town.

After Holmes died in 1911, his family continued to occupy the house until 1960 when it was purchased and restored by Captain and Mrs. Ray Collins.

JOHN PALMER HOUSE 1890: Portland, Oregon

John Palmer, another builder-contractor, completed this Eastlake-detailed, Queen Anne house on Portland's northeast side in 1890, but he only lived in it for a few years. After his wife died in 1894, it was acquired by musicians Oskar and Lotta Hoch and served as headquarters for the Multnomah Conservatory of Music from about 1910 until 1935. More recently it has become the treasure of Mary and Richard Sauter who have devoted themselves to restoring it to its original glory. The exterior is adorned with a variety of ornament including horseshoe-arched braces on the second floor balcony, elaborate gable work, and a spindlework porch frieze. On the inside, the residence is immaculately dressed in period fashions, and contains such rarities as original stained glass from Povey's Studios in Portland, carefully researched wallpapers and lace, and a fine collection of Victorian furniture. Placed on the National Register in 1977, the Palmer House is open for tours by appointment and also serves as a bed and breakfast establishment.

MOREY HOUSE 1890: Redlands, California

The Morey Mansion is justly famous as one of the most spectacular examples of late 19th-century domestic architecture in the country. Built by retired shipbuilder David Morey, it represents the High Victorian sensibility at its most eclectic. There is a little of everything in this amazing house: Italianate brackets and round-headed windows, classical columns and pilasters, Eastlake spindlework, traces of the Stick Style, a Venetian Gothic tower with mansard roof and pointed-arch windows, and—in the Moorish onion-domed tower and Chinese patterning of the porch balustrade—a taste of the mysterious East. And yet beneath all this, the basic Queen Anne Villa is still clearly visible.

Morey and his wife Sarah had retired in 1882 and came to Redlands to grow oranges. Their new enterprise was so successful, however, that they had to retire again in order to build this extraordinary home. It is reported to have cost $20,000, even though Morey, then in his 60s, did much of the work himself. His ship-building talents may have helped in building the onion tower, which is constructed rather like a boat-hull, and he is also responsible for most of the lavishly-carved interior woodwork. The former residence, now the Morey Mansion Bed and Breakfast Inn, is open for tours.

EDWARDS HOUSE 1890: Redlands, California

Perhaps because it is located between Riverside and San Bernardino—two larger neighbors which bore the onus of 20th-century development in the area—Redlands has been able to maintain a substantial part of its architectural past. The Edwards Mansion is one of several large houses in town that date from the period when Southern California's citrus-growing potential was first being developed on a large scale.

It was originally built for James Edwards, a wealthy easterner who became even wealthier marketing the fruit of the orange groves he acquired after his arrival in Redlands in 1881. Who designed his house is not known, but it is believed to have been built from mail-order plans. In addition to its monumental proportions, the mansion is notable for the heavy Eastlake posts and spindles that decorate its porch and balconies, and the open pavilion that surmounts the angled bay at one corner of the facade. After years of neglect in the 20th century, the structure was purchased in 1973 by Donald Wilcott who moved it in sections to its present location, restored it inside and out, and converted it into a restaurant.

WARDNER HOUSE 1890: Bellingham, Washington

"Wardner's Castle" was the residence, for a time, of one of Bellingham's early real estate speculators. At the end of the 1880s Fairhaven (which later became part of Bellingham) was rumored to become the terminus of the Great Northern Railroad, and the whole community was soon marked off like a Monopoly Board. James Wardner arrived in the area in 1889 after making a fortune in Idaho silver and lead and immediately began buying up lots. He also started a sawmill operation, founded a bank, and helped organize local utility companies. Somewhere in the midst of all these activities he found time to commission the design for this house which was constructed the following year.

Longstaff and Black, the architects who designed it, were originally from Boston and had brought some new architectural ideas with them when they came to Bellingham. Their work on the Wardner house has some affinities with the Shingle Style which was then enjoying some popularity in the Northeast. Besides the extensive shingling itself there are some details—the flared wall surface above the gable window and the wide arch of the porte cochere, for instance—that are typical of this sophisticated new stylistic mode. For the most part, however, the design displays a typical Queen Anne taste for diversity and irregularity of form.

Such nuances probably didn't matter much to Wardner who occupied the house for only a year. In 1891 he sold it, along with his other holdings in the area, and was off to South Africa to take part in new mining ventures. Meanwhile the boom in Bellingham had gone bust when Everett was selected as the railroad terminus in the area. His former residence is now a bed and breakfast inn.

FRANK HASTINGS HOUSE 1890: Port Townsend, Washington

Frank Hastings was one of a number of Port Townsend business-men whose real estate investments were riding on a railway that never arrived. He began constructing this house in 1890 but never completed it. By the time the basic shell was finished the economic winter had become so severe that he had to postpone the decorative and interior work for better times. In that year—1890—Hastings was president of the local street car company: three years later the trolley tracks were being torn up for salvage. It was not until after 1904, when the house was auctioned off to one C. A. Olson for $2,500, that it was finally completed.

One can only imagine what it would have looked like if it had been finished as planned. Budgeted at $10,000 in a distinctly florid age, it is likely that it would have been considerably more ornate than it now appears. Still, in basic form, the Hastings House is a virtual paradigm of the corner-towered, Queen-Anne Villa that enjoyed its greatest popularity in the 1890s. In recent years the residence has become a bed and breakfast inn.

KELLER HOUSE c.1890s: Roseburg, Oregon

    Roseburg, now the largest city in Douglas County, Oregon, first assumed importance as an agricultural and timber center in the 1890s, and it retains some interesting Victoriana from this period. In addition to an assortment of restored villas and manses once owned by former mayors and other prominent citizens, the town has managed to preserve some of its late 19th and early 20th-century vernacular housing in more or less original condition. This is somewhat unusual, for such houses are frequently the first to be razed or remodeled in the interests of progress.

    The house pictured here, a rather highly decorated example, shows some obvious influences from the Stick Style: the characteristic patterning is particularly evident in the gables and in the frieze board over the small entry porch. In addition there is a nod to the Italianate in the brackets beneath the eaves. A partially obliterated date panel set at the peak of the front gable suggests that the house was built in the 1890s, and city records indicate that it was moved to its present location in 1912. Apart from this, nothing is known of its early history.

Figure 6: Design No. 37, *The Cottage Souvenir No. 2*

C. D. DRAIN HOUSE c.1891: Drain, Oregon

In relatively remote, inland areas, elaborately styled houses like this one became common only after the arrival of the railroad. Away from the coast, the steel rail was a prerequisite for the new ideas, tools, and stock parts needed to coax rural architecture out of more traditional forms. When it came, the railroad simultaneously fueled local economics and, by offering glimpses of what lay down the track, fanned the desires of the rising middle class for fashionably stylish housing.

Drain, Oregon, was founded in 1872 when C. D. Drain Sr., a former homesteader and state senator, donated sixty acres of Douglas County land to the Oregon and California Railroad "in consideration of establishing a station . . . and laying out a town to be called 'Drain'." In the twenty years that followed, the town flourished as a railway shipping point and timber center, and the Drain family profited from their land interests and the general store C. D. Sr. had established. In the early 90s his son, C. D. Jr., and daughter-in-law, Anna, evidently felt prosperous enough to build this residence which a local newspaper described as "the finest and most costly ever built in Douglas County."

In form it is another rendition of that old favorite, the corner-towered Queen Anne that dotted America from coast to coast by the end of the century. This particular example is especially interesting as a pattern-book house: its plans were ordered from George F. Barber's architectural firm in Knoxville, Tennessee. Whether they were expressly commissioned by the Drain family or not is unclear however. In either case, "Design No. 37" is identified as the "Residence of C. D. Drain" in Barber's *Cottage Souvenir No. 2* (fig. 6). In addition, at least one other version of the house—the Bulloch Home in Eureka Springs, Arkansas—was constructed on the same design. The Drain Mansion, as it is known locally, is in use today as an office of the Douglas County school board.

WELLER HOUSE c.1891: Los Angeles, California

This well-preserved house in Angelino Heights raises some interesting questions about the dissemination of design ideas in the late Victorian period. It looks as if it could have been based on a design (fig. 7) included in G. F. Barber's *Cottage Souvenir No. 2.* (1891), but there are difficulties with this idea. One is that the Weller residence is generally assumed to have been built in the late 1880s, several years before the Barber design appeared in print. Another is that there are more than enough departures between the house and the design to raise some doubts. A comparison of the Los Angeles house with a more or less literal rendering of "Design No. 56" built in Klamath Falls, Oregon (pp. 168–169) is as interesting for the differences it reveals as for the similarities. It seems clear that if Barber's pattern-book design figured at all in the construction of the Weller House, it was substantially modified somewhere along the way.

GOELLER HOUSE c.1905: Klamath Falls, Oregon

In more remote locations in the West, as elsewhere in the United States, the later Victorian Styles continued in fashion well into the twentieth century. This house, for example, was built nearly fifteen years after its plan first appeared as "Design No. 56" (fig. 7) in G. F. Barber's *Cottage Souvenir No. 2.*

Its original owners, Fred Goeller and his wife Alice, had come to Klamath Falls (or Linkville as it was then called) from Kansas in 1891. Their idea was to raise cattle, but Goeller became the operator of a sash and door planing mill instead and built their home with the skills he acquired on the job. Besides supervising the construction personally he was responsible for most of the finer carpentry work himself, including some ornate interior finishing. The furniture, fixtures, and all the hardwood for the inside of the house are reported to have been brought from California (presumably from the nearest railhead) by mule team.

Except that it is reversed in plan, the Goeller House follows Barber's design more or less faithfully and is particularly interesting in comparison to the Weller House in Los Angeles (pp. 166–167) which seems to be a freer rendering of some of the same basic ideas.

Figure 7: Design No. 56, *The Cottage Souvenir No. 2*

F. W. JAMES HOUSE 1891: Port Townsend, Washington

After his arrival in Port Townsend from England in 1853, Francis Wilcox James worked at a variety of jobs including lighthouse keeper and customs inspector. By the time this house was ready for occupancy, however, he had advanced himself to the position of "Capitalist"—as he was listed on the local tax rolls. In the interim, he had become a store owner and acquired an interest in at least one of the commercial buildings that sprang up in Port Townsend in the late 1880s. Unlike some others in his job category he seems to have weathered the financial storms of the early 1890s quite nicely and is reported to have gone to his final reward a rich man.

The house shown here, which he built for his retirement, is basically Queen Anne, but of a type more akin to the boxy English prototypes of the style than to American developments in the picturesque villa mode. Still, it exhibits a number of features commonly associated with the style. These include an asymmetrical facade, complex roof silhouette, varied surface textures, and a bay that springs out of the second floor balcony almost as if it wanted to be a turret. In addition, the interior woodwork is said to be the most sumptuous in Port Townsend. Recently restored, the James House is now a bed and breakfast inn.

J. C. SAUNDERS HOUSE 1891: Port Townsend, Washington

Set on a hill with a commanding view of Puget Sound, this large shingled villa was built just as Port Townsend's final boom was going bust. James C. Saunders, its original owner, arrived in town in the late 1880s, became president of a local bank, and (like almost every other man of means in Port Townsend) began speculating in real estate. Perhaps because he had been appointed customs collector just as the economic storm was beginning, he managed better than most of his contemporaries to survive its immediate effects. When his commission expired in 1898, however, he lost the house to foreclosure and left town.

The design, by a local architect, Edward A. Batwell, is rather more sophisticated than most of the other residences built in Port Townsend in the same period. Although essentially a restatement of the familiar Queen Anne Villa form, it seems to be engaged in a conscious exploration of some new ideas. The gable on one side of the house, for example, is considerably broader than was then customary—large enough, in fact, to accommodate an entire balcony; and, as if to compensate, the tower on the opposite side has shrunk to a mere turret. In addition, the walls have begun to adopt some of the curvilinear shapes of the Shingle Style, and some other features, like the roof dormer, seem to be flirting with the Colonial Revival. To get a better sense of the extent of these changes, see the Hastings House (pp. 160–161) which was built in Port Townsend only a year before this example.

GACHES HOUSE 1891: La Connor, Washington

La Connor, if one can believe the stories, was a town where men paid due homage to their wives. First settled in 1868, it was called "Swinomish" after the Indian tribe that originally inhabited the area. However, John Connor, one of its first residents, renamed the town in honor of his wife, Louise A. Connor. Later George Gaches, an Englishman who had bought out Connor's dry goods store, built the wooden castle shown here for *his* wife, Louisa, who is said to have been homesick for the style and comforts of a proper English house.

The result is indeed English in some respects, but owes as much to New World traditions as to British ones. Its heavy stick work, steep gables, and tower suggest that it is a sort of half-timbered Tudor castle of wood—an architectural chimera that never inhabited the British Isles but was very much at home in the eclectic American wilderness. The house was partially destroyed by fire in 1973, but has been faithfully restored and is now open to the public.

GRAY HOUSE 1891: Santa Cruz, California

Blessed with great natural beauty, Santa Cruz was a popular vacation spot as early as the 1860s, and by the turn of the century it was enjoying its heyday as a seaside resort—an identification it has never entirely lost. Its out-of-the-way location, moreover, did little to encourage industrial expansion during the 20th century. As a consequence, many of the residences that date from the town's period as a late Victorian seaside community are still with us today. The example shown here was originally built for a Captain W. W. Gray in 1891 and was later purchased by Judge Lucas F. Smith, who had acquired a considerable reputation as an Indian fighter and frontier district attorney before coming to California.

As in other medium-sized towns on the West Coast, Santa Cruz residences tended to be designed by builders rather than schooled architects. With the notable exception of W. H. Weeks, who was trained at a technical institute, most of the town's *de facto* architects were men who had learned their profession by direct experience on the job. The Gray House, for example, a fine exponent of the Queen Anne Style, was the work of Le Baron R. Olive, a Canadian "carpitect" who apprenticed with his father and later worked as a construction supervisor. How many houses he designed and built during the Santa Cruz phase of his career in the 1880s and 90s is anyone's guess, but at least six of them, including the Gray House, are still standing today.

BETTNER HOUSE 1892: Riverside, California

The "Riverside Heritage House," as it is now known, was originally built by Catherine Bettner, the widow of a wealthy orange grower. The Bettners had come to California from New York in 1877 for health reasons, and James Bettner, who was originally trained as a civil engineer, quickly achieved success in the citrus industry. Nonetheless, he died some years later, and his grief-stricken widow commissioned this new residence shortly after his passing. She is said to have wanted to remove herself as quickly as possible from their former home and its sad memories.

The design, by John Walls of the Los Angeles firm of Morgan & Walls, is still basically Queen Anne, but like the Saunders House (pp. 172–173) it seems to be making a tentative exploration of some of the newer architectural fashions that were then coming into vogue. The patterned shingles and inward-curving windows of the upper story show the influence of the Shingle Style, while other details like the centered entryway and classically inspired posts are suggestive of the Colonial Revival.

Recently restored inside and out by a volunteer group, the Riverside Museum Associates, the former Bettner House is now listed on the National Register and is open to the public.

Figure 8: Design No. 21, *The Cottage Souvenir No. 2*

SULLIVAN HOUSE 1892: La Connor, Washington

Michael Sullivan, who owned this house originally, was one of the first farmers in the Skagit Valley to dike and drain the marshes near La Connor. As a result he obtained superior farmland, produced record crops of hay and oats, and helped make the area one of the premier agricultural centers in Washington. The house stands on a granite foundation and is constructed entirely of cedar from nearby Camano Island. In style it is a relatively modest member of the Stick-Eastlake-Queen Anne family with such typical embellishments as gable ornaments, gig-cut corner brackets on the bay window, and turned spindlework on the porch. It is probable that Sullivan built the house himself, but no certain information on who designed it has yet surfaced. It bears more than passing resemblance to a design published in *The Cottage Souvenir No. 2.* (fig. 8), however, so it may qualify as yet another pattern-book house by the Knoxville mail-order architect George Franklin Barber.

WILLIAM ANDREWS HOUSE 1892: Napa, California

Napa was settled by a wave of settlers who followed on the heels of the gold seekers who came to California in 1849. Its location at the heart of one of the premier wine districts in the state has helped sustain it in relative prosperity, and it has managed to maintain a fair sampling of its 19th-century architecture. This house in the Queen Anne mode has attained moderate fame for the elaborate decoration that virtually covers it. The ornament is mainly Eastlake and ranges from the turned balusters, posts, and spindles of the porch to the diamondwork patterning and gilded sunburst in the front gable. Some identical decorative fixtures can be seen in the Shwarz-Birnheim House (pp. 194–195). The design is credited to Luther Turton, an architect responsible for several other notable Victorians in town, and it was built for William Andrews, a miller and grocer originally from England who arrived in Napa in the 1860s.

183

NUNAN HOUSE 1892: Jacksonville, Oregon

Figure 9: Design No. 143, *The Cottage Souvenir Revised and Enlarged*

By the 1890s Jacksonville had begun to stagnate. The gold that had started the town off with a boom in 1851 soon began to play out. The easier pickings were gone by the 1860s, and in 1877 an English traveller noted that the returns had diminished to the point that only the Chinese were still willing to work for them. Moreover in the 1880s the railroad, which played such an important role in the fates of small communities everywhere, bypassed the former gold town—in effect handing the reins of government and commerce over to neighboring Medford. Jacksonville, which had once been the leading community in the Rogue River Valley, was on the road to extinction. Nevertheless, in the final decade of the 19th century Jeremiah Nunan, a wealthy dry-goods merchant, built this elaborately styled residence as a gift for his wife and, perhaps, as an affirmation of his faith in the continued prosperity of the town.

The house is based on a pattern-book design by the prolific Knoxville architect, George F. Barber. It appeared as design No. 143 (fig. 9) in *The Cottage Souvenir, Revised and Enlarged,* which he published in 1892 as a follow-up to his earlier books. That the house is still very much in the Queen Anne tradition is evidenced by its elaborate roof and wall forms and the general complication of its ornamental details. The classical columns on the porch and balconies and the Roman arch in the chimney, however, are harbingers of two new styles—the Colonial Revival and the Richardsonian Romanesque. The distinctive buttressed chimney with inset window is, by the way, something of a Barber trademark: it appears in a number of houses attributed to him in various parts of the country.

As for Jacksonville, it never recovered the momentum of its earliest years, but in the late 1960s new life was breathed into the community when its wealth of 19th-century architecture was discovered by preservationists: the whole town was declared a National Historic site in 1969. The Nunan House was purchased by Richard Lucier and Jay Fuller, two Southern California expatriates who accomplished the immaculate restoration shown here. Although the house is a private residence, it is open for tours.

184

GAMWELL HOUSE 1892: Bellingham, Washington

Though some of the examples included in this book might suggest otherwise, the truth is that most of the really extravagant houses of the Victorian period have vanished. Large cities, where they were most often built, turned out to be just the places where they were also most likely to fall to progress. San Francisco excepted, most of the larger cities on the West Coast retain only pale shadows of the lavish mansions that once dominated their streets. However, in smaller towns that made their last bids for major status in the 19th century, there are occasional survivors that suggest something of the true opulence of the period.

An example is the Gamwell House designed by the Boston architects Longstaff and Black. Roland G. Gamwell, had commissioned the pair to design the Fairhaven Hotel in what later became a part of Bellingham, and they stayed in town long enough to design his and a number of other important residences. Although they were already conversant with the sophisticated Shingle Style (as evidenced by their work in the Wardner House, pp. 158–159), they have taken a half step backwards here to demonstrate their command of the late Victorian eclectic idiom. This example is restless in its articulation of exterior space, and in the multiplication of such features as balconies and verandas. Yet for all its complexity, it has an integrated, almost organic look. Unruly elements have been unified by the bowed curves that recur throughout the composition and by the tower with its beetling carapace that presides over the entire structure.

Vintage photographs indicate that similarly appointed houses on an even larger scale once dominated cities like Seattle, Portland, and Los Angeles. These are mostly gone today, and even San Francisco seems to have lost many of the more audacious products of its late Victorian past. The Gamwell House is one of a small group of survivors that point to an order of eccentricity that has almost entirely disappeared from the urban scene.

CHARLES EISENBEIS HOUSE 1892: Port Townsend, Washington

The fascination with medieval castles that expressed itself in so much of the architecture of the Victorian era sometimes gave rise to structures that actually resembled the original models. The Charles Eisenbeis House is a case in point. Designed and constructed by A. S. Whiteway, it was the home of a former Prussian baker who arrived in the United States in 1858 and began accumulating a fortune by supplying bread and crackers to the ships that put into Port Townsend. From these humble beginnings he eventually became the first mayor of the town and developed a personal empire that included holdings in stores, banks, a brewery, local construction, and, of course, real estate.

By the time he was ready to build this monument to his own success, however, many of his business associates had gone down in ruin, and Eisenbeis' own resources were sorely depleted. A hotel he financed in anticipation of the fabled Port Townsend railway never opened, and the interests he held in downtown office buildings had become almost worthless. Nevertheless, he went ahead with his plans for this residence with its distinctly regal overtones. How many chances, after all, does a German baker get to build a castle of his own?

Constructed of exposed brick from Eisenbeis' own foundry, the mansion was stuccoed-over in the mid 1920s when it was acquired for use as a retreat by the Jesuit order. It was in this period that the mansard-roofed wing (far left) was added to the original structure and that the house acquired a new name: "Manresa Hall," which in turn became "Manresa Castle." The former residence is now an inn and is open for tours.

Figure 10: From *Detail, Cottage and Constructive Architecture*

KEYES HOUSE 1892: Bellingham, Washington

This elegant house appears to be based on a design included in *Detail, Cottage, and Constructive Architecture,* a pattern book published by A. J. Bicknell & Co. in several editions in the 1870s and 80s. It was built by Phillip M. Isensee, a contractor who also served as treasurer of the City of New Whatcom—until he was imprisoned for embezzlement. It was later acquired by a physician, William Keyes, who used it as a clinic, and it is now the home of the Montesssori School in Bellingham.

Stylistically it is a High Victorian adaptation of earlier Italianate houses: except for its steep roof most of its details are similar to those of more traditional examples. In type, moreover, it is what Herbert Gottfried and Jan Jennings have termed the "gabled-ell cottage"—a cross-gabled, "L"-shaped house with a porch in the nook created by the projecting wing. This form was a sort of cross between the narrow town house and the more spacious country villa. This particular design, which Bicknell credited to D. B. Provoost of Elizabeth, New Jersey (fig. 10), is, in fact, specifically designated as a "Design for Suburban Residence."

As might be expected, there are some differences between the plan that appeared in the book and the house as it was actually constructed. The arched gable braces are less ornate in the flesh than in the drawing, and some other departures are apparent—the patterned shingles in the gables and the treatment of the porch roof for example. However, in most respects the realization in wood and stone follows Provoost's design fairly closely. Since there is no suggestion that Bicknell & Co. commonly sold plans through the mail, it seems likely that Isensee based his own working drawings on those provided in the pattern book.

To judge from an admittedly limited sampling, the Bicknell volume may have been a fairly popular source of design ideas on the West Coast. The same plan seen here was the basis of another builder's residence, the Albert W. Ferguson House in Astoria (1886); and the McPheters House in Santa Cruz (pp. 74–75) may have derived from another design in the same book.

LAYTON HOUSE 1892: Eureka, California

Hillsdale Street in Eureka has gained renown for the quality and range of the architecture displayed in its single block. Of particular interest are a number of tall, relatively narrow, "gabled-ell" residences—in essence, expanded versions of the town houses popular in San Francisco. Most were the work of local builders rather than architects, and while all have rather similar plans, each has individual touches and varying stylistic roots that set it apart from its neighbors.

The Layton residence is one of several houses on the street that were constructed by a builder named A. A. Redmond. Some of its more obvious features include Stick-Italianate brackets, a false-front gable, and just a touch of Eastlake decoration. In contrast to the simpler bay-front town house, its floor plan has assumed a definite "L" shape, and the squared bay on the projecting wing (or "ell") extends the structure even further toward the street. This example invites comparison with the Keyes and Torrey Houses (pp. 190–191, 193) which, though they have very different detailing, are quite similar in plan.

A. W. TORREY HOUSE 1893: Eureka, California

Though known by the name of one of its longest occupants, this house was originally constructed as the residence of yet another builder-contractor, F. Mowry. Although the neighboring Layton House, (p. 192) still shows strong Stick and Italianate influences, this example, built only a year later, has leaped decisively into the Queen Anne. Characteristic touches include: a boxed-off gable with patterned shingles and rows of Eastlake "buttons," belts of rectangles which mark the division of floors, stained-glass panels which frame the upper half of the front window, and, of course, the exotic horseshoe arches, and sumptuous, almost musical spindlework.

The plan, again, is the familiar "gabled-ell" configuration with a porch filling the nook created by the projecting wing. In this example the edges of the ell have been cut away, so that the front facade looks like a town house with an outsized bay. Another residence next door follows an identical plan (though its decorative details are quite different) and a similar, but altered version of the same design can be seen in the Young-Larson House (pp. 218–219). It appears that Mowry was responsible for all three residences, but in any event all this serves to illustrate the late Victorian tendency to produce "unique" designs by mixing and matching pre-existing elements—both structural and decorative—in new combinations.

SHWARZ-BIRNHEIM HOUSE 1893: Napa, California

This lavishly decorated house was originally the home of Minnie Birnheim, nee Shwarz, the daughter of the owner of the largest hardware store in Napa. Its combination of Queen Anne and Eastlake decorative elements was common in California houses built in the period; and the particular ornament used here invites comparison with the Andrews House (pp. 182–183). Note for example the diaper-work patterning applied in the front gables, the extended brackets that frame the upper windows, the gilded sunburst panels, and the shingle cladding. That some of this decoration seems to be identical in both houses suggests that it may have been purchased in prefabricated form either from local craftsmen or through a catalogue.

Another common motif from the period can be seen in the thin lines that connect the round disks (or "paterae") set into the gable boards. By comparison to the more elaborate gable dressings of earlier examples like the J. Milton Carson House (pp. 100–101), the patterning seen here is considerably simplified—an indication that it was passing out of fashion. Stained or "flashed" glass was also typical in the 1890s. The panels in the canted, corner bay seem to be original, but the glass in the other windows may have been added at some later date. The Shwarz-Birnheim House is now a bed and breakfast inn aptly named "La Belle Epoque."

GRAY-HACKETT HOUSE 1893: Oregon City, Oregon

As one of the oldest American communities on the Pacific side of the mountains, Oregon City is heir to a rich legacy of 19th-century building. Founded in the 1830s by representatives of the British Hudson's Bay Company, it soon became the locus of American settlement in the Oregon Territory and remained important throughout the pioneer period. Although post-World War II suburbanization and commercial encroachment exacted a considerable toll on its historic resources, the town has maintained a representative sampling of its architecture—including some rare survivors from the Federal, Greek, and Gothic periods. The house pictured here belongs to a later generation of buildings but nonetheless retains a feeling of the rustic, pioneer origins of the community.

Built for George Gray, a schoolteacher from Indiana, and his wife Dora, the structure is essentially a rectangular frame house overlayed with stylish embellishments. The canted, tower-like bay with its second-story balcony and truncated pyramidal roof is the most obvious of these, but a bit of stick work, some patterned shingling, and a modest spindle course beneath the roof of the porch are also in evidence. To judge by the design alone the house was probably the work of a local carpenter-builder. But it is in any case typical of the tendency of Oregon City houses to enliven vernacular forms with high-style borrowings.

After the Grays sold the house in 1908 it was acquired by Erwin C. Hackett, a deputy sheriff who also served a term as town mayor. In recent years it has been restored and converted for commercial use.

Figure 11: Design No. 27, *The Cottage Souvenir Revised and Enlarged*

BREHAUT HOUSE 1893: Alameda, California

Because it occupies a small island of its own, Alameda has managed to maintain its original residential character better than most other communities in the sprawling East Bay. Many of its neighborhoods are substantially unchanged since they were developed in the booms of the 1880s and 90s. Moreover, the overall quality of the housing is quite high. Some notable architects are represented in the town, and local builders seem to have made particularly extensive use of pattern-book designs and prefabricated fixtures. In addition, the community's residents seem to have been aware of the value of historic preservation from the start. As a result of all this, Alameda has one of the highest concentration of elaborate well-preserved Victorians on the West Coast.

The Thomas Brehaut residence, an especially fine example of the town's architecture, illustrates some of these points. Immaculately maintained, it has never required restoration and stands today essentially as it was built. In its nearly one hundred-year history it has changed hands only twice, and one of its current owners has occupied it for nearly 50 years.

The house is based on a pattern-book design by George F. Barber (fig. 11) with modifications by a local practitioner, Charles H. Shaner. The central tower and dual entry porch with its open pavilion are elements of the published plan, while the more or less symmetrical wings are Shaner's contribution—unless, of course, they too derived from a stock design source. The residence, which represents the Queen Anne in a later eclectic phase, is said to have cost only $4,000 to build—an indication that high style had become considerably more egalitarian than in the past.

199

HASARD HOUSE c.1894: Drain, Oregon

This house was once the residence of Charles E. Hasard who originally came to the Umpqua Valley to work as a carpenter for the Oregon & California Railroad. He later farmed for several years and in 1902 was appointed U.S. land commissioner in the area. He is said to have built the house himself, and it has been theorized that it was more or less directly inspired by the Drain Mansion (pp. 164–165), the first elaborately styled Victorian constructed in the rather small community that bears its founder's name. If so, Hasard may have drawn from the same design source—the George F. Barber firm in Knoxville, Tennessee—that served C. D. Drain Jr. Though it does not explicitly follow any published Barber plan, Hasard's residence resembles "Design No. 33" in *The Cottage Souvenir No. 2* in some of its decorative details. It may be, then, that this design, and perhaps some others, inspired his own.

WRIGHT-MOOERS HOUSE 1894: Los Angeles, California

Built by a contractor, Frank L. Wright, this house was later purchased by Frederick Mitchell Mooers, a former bookkeeper who was one of the discoverers of the famous Yellow Aster mine in California. Originally from Ithaca, New York, Mooers worked at a desk job in New York City until, overcome by wanderlust, he headed west one day. For several years he alternately prospected and worked as a newspaper reporter, but in 1895, he discovered a literal mountain of gold scarcely 150 miles from Los Angeles. Mooers was inclined to dismiss the hardships of gold-mining itself, but in the aftermath of his discovery he found that he had to deal "with dangers that are greater than any encountered on the desert... the most outrageous blackmailing schemes ever conceived by man or devil."

Notwithstanding the machinations of "the greatest scheming legal brains on the Pacific Coast," Mooers and his partners emerged from the Mojave with their claim intact, and he repaired to Los Angeles where he purchased this house. It represents the Queen Anne in a confusingly eclectic stage. Nothing is known of its architect, so the range of influences at work in the busy facade have to speak for themselves. Some of these are decidedly Middle-Eastern—the onion-domed tower with its elfin-eared dormers most obviously. In addition the paired colunnettes and heavy arched porch entry may have been influenced by Moorish antecedants. There is also some Eastlake ornament here and there, and the teardrop curve that frames the balcony in dynamic asymmetry suggests something of the spirit of the European Art Nouveau movement. Whatever its sources, the design is highly original, and the uniqueness of the house has been recognized by the City of Los Angeles which has declared it an Historic-Cultural Monument.

203

HECETA HOUSE 1894: Oregon Coast

Named for Bruno Heceta, a Spanish explorer who charted the area in 1775, Heceta Head juts into the ocean about half way up the Oregon coast. It is a lonely and beautiful spot, and, as thousands of tourist photos attest, provides one of the most picturesque settings for a lighthouse anywhere in the United States. The light tower itself, with its small attached duty station, stands at the furthest extension of the rocky point. The house shown here, which once sheltered the keepers of the light, is set behind a knoll which provides protection from the sometimes brisk off shore breezes.

Heceta House, as it is now called, was one of two cottages built on the site when the lighthouse was commissioned in the early 1890s. It is a duplex (or more properly a double house) that once served as living quarters for the assistant light keepers and their families. A similar, single family dwelling was built for the head keeper but was razed in the 1940s. The original outpost also included a barn and outbuildings for the animals that helped sustain the little community in what remained a somewhat isolated location until well into the 20th century. The entire station was constructed for about $180,000.

The house was built by a Portland construction firm from what may have been a standard plan: an identical house, since razed, was erected at the Umpqua Light Station south of Reedsport. As signaled by the multi-textured wall surfaces, porch spindlework, and modest gable ornament, its style is restrained, government-issue Queen Anne. The symmetrical facade and the fanlight on the side wall, however, suggest a leaning toward the Colonial Revival which later became the dominant style for official maritime architecture.

The last lighthouse keeper departed when the station was fully automated in 1963, and Heceta House was subsequently taken over by the National Forest Service. It has since become a restoration project of Lane Community College and is open for tours by appointment.

PAUL HOUSE c.1894: Oakland, California

This towered Queen Anne perched on a hill in east Oakland is named for a family that occupied it for most of a century, but it was originally built as the home of W. H. Gregory, a real estate agent who may also have been a builder-speculator. It has been dated as early as 1889, but other sources suggest that it was actually constructed somewhat later, which indeed seems more in accord with some elements of its design. The boxed-off front gable, for example, and flared tower (almost Richardsonian in its proportions) are more characteristic of the 1890s than of the previous decade. Some of the differences between this heavily shingled phase of the Queen Anne and its earlier incarnation in Eastlake finery may become apparent by comparing this example with the J. Milton Carson House (pp. 100–101) which presents a rather similar face to the street.

The neighborhood in which the Paul House was built, by the way, was originally called Brooklyn, and was covered with redwoods—though these were soon logged off. It was eventually incorporated by its larger neighbor, Oakland, and came into its own in the 1880s and 90s as a "desirable suburban location" for the homes of San Francisco and East Bay businessmen.

JULIUS LEE HOUSE 1894: Watsonville, California

Trained in architecture at the Brinker Institute in Denver, William Henry Weeks (1865–1935) first practiced in Wichita, Kansas, but soon moved to California. Before opening an office in San Francisco in 1904, he worked out of Watsonville for nearly a decade and became one of the leading architects in the area. The residence shown here (built for Julius Lee, a lawyer and Santa Cruz County district attorney) is thought to be his first commission in town, but it already contains some of the ideas he later employed in his design for the Morris Tuttle Mansion (pp. 228–229). In some respects, indeed, the Lee House is even more sophisticated. "Up to date in every way and . . . entirely new to this section in its architectural design," is how a local paper characterized the house shortly after it was completed.

What the writer found so novel was essentially the familiar Queen Anne overladen with borrowings from more recent architectural trends. The older style is still apparent both in the overall configuration of the house and in details like the corner tower and the vestigial spindlework that decorates the second-floor balcony. But there are some new touches as well: the porch is now equipped with modillions and paired classical columns from the Colonial Revival, the attic window flares inward in the manner of the Shingle Style, and the porch frieze, dormer gable, and tower are adorned with Adam applique. In addition, elements that once might have enjoyed more autonomy have now become part of a unified, overall plan. The stout tower, for example, has been smoothly integrated into the rest of the structure, and the main and porch roofs have become a single unit. All in all, very modern—particularly for a small town in a rural area.

DR. K. A. J. MACKENZIE HOUSE 1894: Portland, Oregon

Like Longstaff and Black who moved to Bellingham in the early 1890s, William Whidden and Ion Lewis were a pair of Boston-trained architects who brought fashionable eastern styles with them when they set up a practice in Portland. Though perhaps best known for their work in the Colonial Revival idiom, they designed this residence in a style that drew its name and some of its distinction from one of the greatest 19th-century American architects: Henry Hobson Richardson.

Richardson, who had studied at the Ecole des Beaux-Arts in Paris, almost singlehandedly forged a new style in American architecture. Drawing on Romanesque precedents, which he thought combined the best elements of both Gothic and Roman models, he created a series of bold, simple designs that became the stylistic source for many commercial and public buildings constructed in the United States from the 1880s until the end of the century. In the realm of domestic architecture, the "Richardsonian Romanesque," which in its purest form required relatively expensive masonry construction, was never widely popular, but it did gain some currency as a high style for the well-to-do.

Though not an entirely pure example, the Mackenzie House, which was originally the home of a distinguished Portland surgeon, contains a number of features commonly associated with the style. The massive stone construction, the fat tower with its conical roof, and the rounded Roman arches that form an arcaded porch seem to have been directly inspired by Richardson's prototypes. The eyebrow dormer and the imbricate patterning of the second story, however, are more characteristic of the Shingle Style.

211

PORT HOUSE 1895: Salem, Oregon

This house was designed by the young architect William C. Knighton for Dr. Luke Port, an English-born druggist and land speculator who lived in Salem for a number of years. The rambling design with its porch extensions and balconies creates a free-flowing interaction between interior and exterior space that is typical of the Queen Anne Style. This particular house, however, is decorated less extravagantly than many of its cousins. Perhaps Knighton was already demonstrating the capacity for restraint that later helped him acquire the post of Oregon State Architect, a position in which he designed such models of neoclassical sobriety as the State Supreme Court building.

Dr. and Mrs. Port sold the house a year or so after it was built and moved to sunny Southern California. It was purchased in the mid 1920s by Alice and Clifford Brown who commissioned landscape architects Elizabeth Lord and Edith Schryver to design the extensive gardens that now cover the grounds. It was in this period that the estate acquired its current name, "Deepwood." It is now maintained by the city of Salem and is open for tours by the public.

DETACHED ROWHOUSES c.1895: San Francisco, California

In this famous view of the old and the new San Francisco, the town house is seen in its Queen Anne phase. Except that the individual houses are not really attached, this elegant grouping would merit the genteel English term "Terrace," which is sometimes used to designate row houses that function together in an overall design scheme. Constructed by Matthew Kavanaugh, a carpenter-builder, the group is indisputably a unit, but no two houses in it are precisely the same. Variations in porch, gable, and window details, along with different color schemes create individuality within uniformity. It would be most interesting to know which touches were the work of the original builder and which are due to subsequent owners.

QUEEN ANNE TOWN HOUSE
c.1895: San Francisco, California

In general the town house followed the same stylistic evolution as suburban and country houses. From minimal beginnings it picked up Italianate, then Stick, Eastlake, and (as seen in this example from the "Kavanaugh Terrace") Queen Anne detailing. Meanwhile, the early flat-front plan gave way to bay front. The basic San Francisco house type that resulted (seen also in the Sloss and Vollmer Houses pp. 47, 84–85) typically had a small entry porch on one side of the facade and a projecting, two-story bay on the other. This configuration amounts to a narrow, urban version of the "gabled-ell" house more commonly found in the suburbs.

GOLDSMITH HOUSE c.1896 Portland, Oregon

Aside from the surname of its first owner, not much information has yet surfaced on the origins of this house. Nevertheless, it is interesting for the combination of decorative elements it displays. Its busy facade contains allusions to most of the late Victorian Styles. Remnants of stick-work appear in the extended window surrounds and in the thin vertical boards within the gables, Eastlake influences are evident in the carved panels, turned posts, and rows of paterae applied here and there, and there is a hint of the Queen Anne in the flared shingle course that belts the house at its waist. The unusual lathe-cut gable trusses are, however, the most distinctive ornamental features. These are variations on the "King-post" motif—a decorative echo of the structural brace and tie-beam system that supports many a roof. Stylized trusses of this sort were a characteristic feature of the Stick Style but seem to have been much more common in the East than on the West Coast.

YOUNG-LARSON HOUSE c.1896: Eureka, California

"The House of Francis," as it is now known, was originally built by a Eureka family, the Youngs, who occupied it for many years. More recently it was acquired and restored by Mr. and Mrs. Francis Larson, and still later, in 1978, it was moved several blocks from its original site to a new location in Eureka's Old Town district. Since 1982 it has served as a bed and breakfast inn.

Perhaps because it was built entirely of redwood—a material frequently used in Eureka—the house has weathered the passing years rather well. It is reported to have been built in 1893, but its upper floor was remodeled after it was damaged by fire a few years later. An example in the Queen Anne Style, its simple design is enhanced by Eastlake ornament and a three-arched, "Palladian" porch entry that reiterates the curves of the cutaway front wing. That identical decoration graces the front of a two-story house on Eureka's Hillsdale Street suggests that these items were stock ornamental fixtures applied by a local carpenter-builder. The other house is credited to a contractor named F. Mowry (p. 193), so it would appear that he built this one as well.

SARGENT HOUSE 1896: Salinas, California

Though popular in seaside vacation communities in the Northeast, the Shingle Style never achieved wide acceptance in the rest of the United States. Scattered examples are found in the West, especially in California, but they are rare and usually mixed with other styles. The Sargent House, attributed to William Henry Weeks, who also designed residences for the Tuttle and Lee families in Watsonville (pp. 228–229, 208–209), illustrates the characteristic blending with the Queen Anne that usually occurred when West Coast architects essayed buildings in the new style.

In this example such Queen Anne elements as the corner tower and wide verandah have been reinterpreted in the Shingle manner. The porch, for example, no longer has a roof of its own: it is covered instead by a broad gable that dominates the entire front of the house. The vestigial turret has been half swallowed by a cross gable so that it is scarcely more than an oversized dormer. The classically inspired porch posts and the wave patterning in the front gable—something also seen in the Sessions House in Los Angeles (pp. 124–125)—were also characteristic of the style as it appeared on the West Coast.

Originally the residence of Bradley V. Sargent, who once served as District Attorney for Monterey County, the house has been converted for use as office space.

STEINBECK HOUSE 1897: Salinas, California

Though built and originally owned by one J. J. Connor, this comfortable-looking house is best known as the birthplace and early home of John Steinbeck. His parents purchased it in 1900, a few years before he was born, and he grew up and wrote his first stories and earliest novels in its Queen Anne embrace. It is perhaps typical of the sort of substantial, middle-class dwellings that became common in California valley communities late in the century. There is a hint of the sumptuous in some of the decorative details—brackets, turned posts, spindlework, sunbursts—and a touch of drama in the twin thrusts of the closed gable on the left and the residual turret on the right. However, the overall effect of the solid, horizontal structure is reserved compared to some of the more florid examples of the era. All in all it was probably an ideal residence for John and Olive Steinbeck, he a businessman and Monterey County Treasurer, she a schoolteacher.

As for their son, the Nobel laureate, it seems to have been good for him too. It may be far-fetched to suggest a relationship between writing and architecture, but the house quite simply looks like Steinbeck might have grown up there. It is irresistible to note that in describing his parents' home as "immaculate and friendly . . . grand enough but not pretentious," he might equally have been characterizing his own prose.

The residence has been completely restored in recent years, and is now operated as a restaurant by the Valley Guild, a volunteer service organization.

ROBERT LYTLE HOUSE 1897: Hoquiam, Washington

Set on a hillside, this twenty-room mansion surveys the towns of Aberdeen and Hoquiam as well as Grays Harbor and the surrounding timber country. This area, which was first settled in 1859, then contained some of the densest forests in North America and was at first accessible only by sea. As a result it developed slowly, and it was not until the 1880s that it began to assume importance as a lumber center. From that decade until well into the 20th century Aberdeen and Hoquiam experienced steady growth based on the seemingly unlimited stands of trees that surrounded them. During the period a number of stately mansions began springing up to house the various lumber barons who had arrived on the scene.

One of the latter, Robert Lytle, built what has become known as "Hoquiam's Castle" in a style that is as close to the Richardsonian Romanesque as a lumberman is apt to get. Though primarily of wood construction, the house stands on a raised stone foundation, and there are such typically Romanesque features as an arcaded verandah and a round tower. However, there are also various Queen Anne and Shingle elements in what seems to be, in the final analysis, a typically eclectic turn-of-the-century design. Hoquiam's Castle was restored and refurbished by the Robert Watson family in the early 1970s. It is now listed on the National Register of Historic Places, and, though a private residence, is open for tours.

L. C. MARSHALL HOUSE c.1898: Albany, Oregon

In the last decades of the 19th century Albany prospered as a river and railroad center. But in the 20th it was cut off from the mainstream of progress when U.S. 99 and Interstate 5, the major north-south highways on the West Coast, bypassed the town center by several miles. This had the effect of concentrating new growth elsewhere, leaving much of the original community and many of its vintage homes intact.

The house shown here, one of the town's best examples in the Queen Anne Style, was originally the residence of Lewellyn C. Marshall, president of the Albany Butter & Produce Company. Marshall's parents had come to Oregon from Iowa in 1852 when he was nine years old. His father died shortly after their arrival, and the boy was obliged to take up farm work to help sustain his family. He prospered despite these early hardships, however, and he and his wife eventually became prominent figures in local society.

Their home is perhaps typical of the sort of conservative Queen Anne houses that were often built in the last years of the 19th century. Most of the characteristic features of the style are still in evidence, but some of the more extravagant elements have been toned down. The pavilion at one corner of the wraparound porch, for example, substitutes a touch of whimsy for the full-blown drama of a tower. And the decorative details are relatively subdued by comparison to some earlier examples. The roof silhouette and wall forms, however, are still properly complex. All in all, the house wears the style comfortably, and, unlike the Tuttle House (pp. 228–229), shows no inclination to adopt the neoclassical details that increasingly began to influence Queen Anne design in the late 1890s.

MORRIS TUTTLE HOUSE 1899: Watsonville, California

Though built in California, the Tuttle Mansion may be the ultimate midwestern farmhouse. Morris Tuttle, who commissioned it, was originally from Iowa, but in 1873, when he was 15 years old, he came west with his father's family. He later started his own family and took up farming in the Pajaro Valley southeast of Santa Cruz, and to judge by this enormous house and his reported six children he was evidently quite successful at both enterprises. The mansion, designed by William Henry Weeks, is constructed of such exotic materials as Hungarian ash and Arizona sandstone and is said to have cost $20,000—about $1,000 per room. It illustrates, moreover, some of the changes that overtook the Queen Anne Style in the last years of the 19th century.

In this late example, the villa form has become more solid and conservative and has lost some of the spindly quality that often characterized it in the past. The hints of picturesque drama that remain in the silhouette and overall configuration of the house are overpowered and contained by the massive, ground-hugging structure itself. The corner tower—really more a turret now—has lost some of its independence and is proportionally shorter and stouter than many of its predecessors. The wraparound porch, meanwhile, has acquired some classical details: the turned posts of an earlier era have been replaced by Roman columns, and the entryways are surmounted by pediments.

This phase of the Queen Anne, sometimes called the "Free Classic," shows the influence of neo-classical movements like the Colonial Revival which became increasingly popular in the 1890s and in the first decades of the 20th century. Some gestures in this direction are apparent in some of the earlier residences Weeks designed in Santa Cruz and Watsonville—the Julius Lee House (pp. 208–209) for example—but none of the others offered as large a canvas on which to paint as the Tuttle Mansion. The former residence now serves as an office building.

RING HOUSE 1899: Ferndale, California

Now known as "The Gingerbread Mansion," this spindlework confection was originally built for Hogan J. Ring, a Norwegian doctor who practiced in Ferndale for many years. The rear of the house was enlarged in the 1920s to serve as a hospital, but the front elevation seems to be substantially the same today as when it was first built. The house was restored in the early 1980s by two former San Franciscans, Wendy Hatfield and Ken Torbert, who now operate it as a bed and breakfast.

Evidently Dr. Ring had a taste for cut and turned ornament, for the house is fairly dripping with it. The sunburst, a favorite Victorian motif, gets a particularly good workout. It appears in its older Stick-Eastlake form in the gable dressings, and in a newer, three-dimensional incarnation as part of the lathe-cut porch and balcony work. Elaborate spindlework of this sort was a characteristic decorative feature of many late Queen Anne houses and was the only type of Victorian fancywork that continued to find steady employment—for a few years at least—after the turn of the century.

233

FLIPPIN HOUSE 1900: Clatskanie, Oregon

Thomas J. Flippin was a lumberman who had begun his career as a "skid-greaser" on a bull team at the age of 17. From this humble beginning, he became an independent logger and eventually acquired his own sawmill near Clatskanie, a small town on the Columbia River. Some years later he built this castlelike house for his retirement. Its unusual design has been variously ascribed to Flippin himself and to Markwell & Sons, who appear to have been itinerant builders.

Unlike the Tuttle Mansion (pp. 228–229), which added an overlay of Colonial-Revival detailing to the basic towered Queen Anne Villa form, the Flippin House has taken on a newer, neo-classical configuration. Nevertheless, it retains much of the feeling of the Queen Anne. Colonial influences appear in the classical columns and formal, symmetrical arrangement of the facade, but some sense of the older style is still apparent in the variegated wall surfaces and romantically evocative towers. Though quite individual in style, the house is typical, in a sense, of the eclectic tendencies of the later Victorian period. It now serves as a senior citizens' center and is open for tours.

SHERWOOD HOUSE 1901: Coquille, Oregon

This house with its dramatic four-story tower was constructed for Andrew J. Sherwood, a lawyer and businessman who established himself and his family in the town of Coquille at the close of the 19th century. A timber center a few miles inland from the coast, the community had been incorporated only 15 years previously, and many of the materials for the residence (bricks, hardware, and fixtures) had to be shipped in by steamboat. As might be expected, the wood was milled locally and is said to have been handpicked by Sherwood who supervised the construction personally. Though it does not appear in any of his publications, the design is credited to George F. Barber, whose signature is appended to printed specifications that have survived along with the structure itself.

In plan the house is still very much in the continuum that begins with the Gothic Revival and ends with the Queen Anne, but its decorative features are somewhat more austere than in the past. Some rather fancy spindlework remains, but the surface ornament that covered many similar examples in the 1890s is no longer in evidence. This shift in decorative emphasis corresponds with the tenor of the times. A less effusive, more sober spirit had emerged in the waning years of the 19th century, and by the first year of the 20th it had become a definite trend. Houses based on the old models continued to be built for several years after the turn of the century, but they seldom ventured again into the pure fancy that had characterized Victorian design at its height. Queen Victoria's death in 1901 was the merely symbolic end of an architectural era that had in fact been over for several years.

HOVANDER HOUSE 1903: Ferndale, Washington

This example of Old World Gothic was built by Holan Hovander on land he purchased for a family farm near the Nooksack River which lies roughly between Bellingham and the Canadian border. Hovander was a retired Swedish architect, and the differences between this house and contemporaneous American designs are most interesting. It is hard to say whether he was working in a standard mode of the European Victorian or was attempting a sort of pastiche on some of the styles popular in the United States in the last quarter of the 19th century. In either case the exuberant eccentricity and flair that generally characterized American eclecticism in the late Victorian period is missing here. Instead Gothic, Stick, and Queen Anne elements have been combined in a staid, symmetrical arrangement unusual for this side of the Atlantic. The entire Hovander Homestead was acquired by Whatcom County in the 1970s. It is now a park, and the house is open for tours.

Index to Houses

241

CALIFORNIA

Index to Architects & Builders

Bibliography

American Institute of Architects. Southwestern Oregon Chapter. *Style and Vernacular: A Guide to the Architecture of Lane County, Oregon.* Eugene: Oregon Historical Society, 1983.

Andrews, Wayne. *American Gothic: Its Origins, Its Trials, Its Triumphs.* New York: Random House, 1975.

Architectural Resources Group. *Eureka: An Architectural View.* Eureka Heritage Society Inc., 1987.

Barber, George F. *The Cottage Souvenir No. 2.: A Repository of Artistic Cottage Architecture and Miscellaneous Designs.* Knoxville: S. B. Newman & Co., 1891. Reprint. Introduction by Michael A. Tomlan. Watkins Glen: American Life Foundation, 1982.

Bear, Dorothy and Beth Stebbins. *Mendocino.* Mendocino Historical Research, 1973.

Bicknell, Amos Jackson. *Bicknell's Village Builder: A Victorian Architectural Guidebook.* New York: 1870, 1872. Reprint. Introduction & Commentary by Paul Goeldner. Watkins Glen: American Life Foundation, 1976.

Bicknell, Amos Jackson. *Detail, Cottage, and Constructive Architecture.* New York: Bicknell & Co., 1873, 1881, 1886. Reprint. *Victorian Architecture: Two Pattern Books by A. J. Bicknell and William T. Comstock.* Introduction by John Maas. Watkins Glen: American Life Foundation, 1976.

Brown, Tracey, and Valerie Patton. "The Castle in Drain Oregon." Xeroxed. Drain, Oregon: No date.

Bruegmann, Robert. *Benicia: Portrait of an Early California Town.* San Francisco: 101 Productions, 1980.

Chase, John. *The Sidewalk Companion to Santa Cruz Architecture.* Santa Cruz Historical Society, 1975.

Clark, Rosalind. *Architecture, Oregon Style.* Portland: Professional Book Center, 1983.

Cleveland, Henry, William Backus and Samuel Backus. *American Village Homes.* New York: D. Appleton & Co., 1856, 1869. Reprint. Watkins Glen: American Life Foundation, 1976.

Dennison, Allen T., and Wallace K. Huntington. *Victorian Architecture of Port Townsend, Washington.* Saanichton and Seattle: Hancock House, 1978.

Downing, Andrew Jackson. *The Architecture of Country Houses.* New York: D. Appleton & Co., 1850. Reprint. Introduction by J. Stewart Johnson. New York: Dover, 1969.

Ferndale Museum. *The Victorian Homes of Ferndale.* Ferndale, CA: Ferndale Museum, 2nd ed. 1985.

Finucane, Stephanie. *Heceta House: A Historical and Architectural Survey.* Waldport, Oregon: Lane Community College & U.S. Forest Service.

Foley, Mary Mix. *The American House.* New York: Harper & Row, 1980.

Gault, Vera Whitney. *A Brief History of Astoria, Oregon.* By the author, 1393 Franklin Ave. 97103, 1982.

Gebhard, David and Robert Winter. *Architecture in Los Angeles: A Compleat Guide.* Salt Lake City: Peregrine Smith, 1985.

Gebhard, David, Roger Montgomery, Robert Winter, John Woodbridge and Sally Woodbridge. *A Guide to Architecture in San Francisco & Northern California.* 2nd ed. Salt Lake City: Peregrine Smith, 1976.

Gibbs, Jim. *West Coast Lighthouses: A Pictorial History of the Guiding Lights of the Sea.* Seattle: Superior Publishing Co., 1974.

Gottfried, Herbert and Jan Jennings. *American Vernacular Design: 1870–1940.* New York: Van Nostrand Reinhold, 1985.

Hawkins, William John. *The Grand Era of Cast-Iron Architecture in Portland.* Portland: Binford & Mort, 1976.

Kirker, Harold. *California's Architectural Frontier.* Salt Lake City: Peregrine Smith, 1986.

Knuth, Priscilla. "'Picturesque' Frontier: The Army's Fort Dalles." *Oregon Historical Quarterly.* Dec. 1966 & March 1967.

Lewis, Betty, *W. H. Weeks, Architect.* Fresno: Panorama West, 1985.

McAlester, Virginia and Lee. *A Field Guide to American Houses.* New York: Alfred E. Knopf, 1985.

Newsom, Joseph C. and Samuel. *Picturesque California Homes.* San Francisco: By the authors, 1884. Reprint. Introduction by David Gebhard. Los Angeles: Hennessey & Ingalls, 1978.

Olmsted, Roger and T. H. Watkins with photographs by Morley Baer. *Here Today, San Francisco's Architectural Heritage.* San Francisco: Chronicle Books, 1968.

Reece, Daphne. *Historical Houses of the Pacific Northwest.* San Francisco: Chronicle Books, 1985.

Richey, Elinor. *The Ultimate Victorians of the Continental Side of San Francisco Bay.* Berkely: Howell-North, 1970.

Staples, Lila. "90 Years Later, A Victorian Tale Emerges: William Lacy and the Widow Murdoch." *San Marino News,* 11 April 1985, p. 1.

Turbeville, Daniel. *A Catalog of Historic Bellingham Buildings: 1852–1915.* Bellingham: Municipal Arts Commission, 1977.

Van Kirk, Susie. *Reflections on Arcata's History: Eighty Years of Architecture.* City of Arcata, 1979.

Walters, Jonathan. "Seattle's Oldest House Gets a New Home." *Historic Preservation.* 39:2 (March/April 1987), 72–75.

Woodbridge, Sally, and Roger Montgomery. *A Guide to Architecture in Washington State.* Seattle: University of Washington Press, 1980.

Acknowledgments

The author and publisher would like to thank the numerous people who helped make this book possible. We are particularly grateful to the many Victorian owners who generously shared information about their homes. In addition, the following individuals and groups were especially vital sources of help and information.

Sonja Akerman, City of Ashland, Oregon

American Life Foundation, Watkins Glen, New York

Belvedere-Tiburon Landmarks Society, Tiburon, California

Benicia Capitol State Historic Park, Benicia, California

Calaveras County Historical Society, San Andreas, California

Cultural Heritage Foundation of Southern California Inc.

Kate Daschel, City of Oregon City

Daughters of the Pioneers of Washington

Larry and Katherine Davis

Douglas County Museum, Roseburg, Oregon

Ezra Meeker Historical Society, Puyallup, Washington

The Ferndale Museum, Ferndale, California

Fort Dalles Museum Commission, The Dalles, Oregon

Vera Whitney Gault, Clatsop County Historical Society, Astoria, Oregon

Leonard Garfield, Washington State Office of Archaeology and Historic Preservation

Good Connections: Mendocino, California

Terry Harbour, Douglas County Planning Department, Roseburg, Oregon

Sara Hews, Cultural Heritage Commission, City of Napa

Jerry Jacobson, Planning Department, City of Eugene

Rosalind Clark Keeney, City of Albany, Oregon

Kristina Kennann, University of Oregon

Klamath County Museum, Klamath Falls, Oregon

Marian Ledgerwood, Eureka Heritage Society

Linn County Historical Museum, Brownsville, Oregon

Anna Murphy, California State Office of Historic Preservation

Oregon Historical Society, Portland

Pacific Grove Heritage Society, Pacific Grove, California

Pajaro Valley Historical Association, Watsonville, California

Elisabeth Potter, Oregon State Office of Historic Preservation

Save Our Heritage Organisation, San Diego, California

Southern Oregon Historical Society, Jacksonville, Oregon

A. K. Smiley Public Library, Redlands, California

Michael A. Tomlan, Cornell University

T. Michael Ward

Illustration Credits

Figures 2, 3, 5, 6, 7, 8, 10, 11 courtesy The American Life Foundation, Box 349 Watkins Glen, New York 14891; Figure 4, courtesy Hennessey & Ingalls, Santa Monica, CA; Figure 9, courtesy Michael A. Tomlan, Cornell University.

About the Author

Kenneth Naversen is a freelance photographer and writer whose work has appeared in many national publications. He is a former recipient of an Art Critics Fellowship from the National Endowment for the Arts and holds a masters degree in Art and Photography. For the past ten years he has been working as a commercial and architectural photographer based in Los Angeles, but he is currently working out of Eugene, Oregon.